Top 25 locator map
(continues on inside
back cover)

◄

TwinPack
Me___ca

TONY KELLY

writes
_ers and
_alising in
_e outdoors.
travelling he lives
nea_ _ambridge with his wife
and young son. Among his
other books are AA *Essential*
Mallorca, *Essential* Costa
Brava and *Spiral* Gran Canaria.

If you have any comments
or suggestions for this guide
you can contact the editor at
Twinpacks@theAA.com

AA Publishing
Find out more about AA Publishing and
the wide range of travel publications and
services the AA provides by visiting our
website at *www.theAA.com/bookshop*

Contents

life *5–12*

A Personal View *6–7*
Menorca in Figures *8*
People of Menorca *9*

A Chronology *10–11*
Best of Menorca *12*

how to organise your time *13–22*

Walks & Drives *14–19*
Finding Peace & Quiet *20–21*

What's On *22*

top 25 sights *23–48*

1. Alaior *24*
2. Barranc d'Algendar (Algendar Gorge) *25*
3. Binibeca Vell *26*
4. Cala d'Algaiarens *27*
5. Cala En Turqueta *28*
6. Cala Macarella *29*
7. Cala Morell *30*
8. Cala Pregonda *31*
9. Cala Santa Galdana *32*
10. Cales Coves *33*
11. Ciutadella *34*
12. Ciutadella's Museu Municipal *35*
13. Ciutadella's Plaça des Born *36*
14. Es Migjorn Gran *37*
15. Ferreries *38*
16. Fornells *39*
17. Maó *40*
18. Maó's Església del Carme *41*
19. Maó Harbour *42*
20. Maó's Plaça de S'Esplanada *43*
21. Monte Toro *44*
22. Naveta des Tudons *45*
23. S'Albufera des Grau *46*
24. Son Bou *47*
25. Torre d'en Galmés *48*

Index *92–93*

About this book *4*

best *49–60*

Remote Beaches *50*
Viewpoints & Scenic Spots *51*
Historic Buildings *52*
Town & City Sights *53*
Beach Resorts *54*
Archaeological Sites *55*

Children's Attractions *56–57*
Unusual Outdoor Attractions *58*
Free Attractions *59*
Places to Have Lunch
  by the Sea *60*

where to... *61–83*

EAT
In Maó *62–63*
In Ciutadella *64–65*
Around the Island *66–69*

STAY
In Maó & Ciutadella *70*
Around the Island *71–73*

SHOP
Food & Drink *74*

Arts, Books & Gifts *75*
Leather & Jewellery *76–77*

BE ENTERTAINED
Art Galleries, Cinemas &
  Theatres *78*
Music & Nightlife *79*
Discos *80*
Spectator & Participatory
  Sport *81*
Watersports *82–83*

practical matters *85–91*

Before You Go *86*
When You Are There *87–90*
Public Transport *89*

Personal Safety *90*
Health *90*
Language *91*

Credits, Acknowledgements and Titles in this Series *94*

About this book

KEY TO SYMBOLS

- ✚ Grid reference to the Top 25 locator map
- ✉ Address
- ☎ Telephone number
- 🕘 Opening times
- 🍴 Restaurant or café on premises or near by
- Ⓜ Nearest underground (tube) station
- 🚆 Nearest railway station
- 🚌 Nearest bus route
- ⛴ Nearest riverboat or ferry stop
- ♿ Facilities for visitors with disabilities
- ✋ Admission charge
- ⬄ Other nearby places of interest
- ❓ Other practical information
- ▶ Indicates the page where you will find a fuller description
- ℹ Tourist information

TwinPack Menorca is divided into six sections to cover the six most important aspects of your visit to Menorca. It includes:

- The author's view of the island and its people
- Suggested walks and excursions
- The Top 25 Sights to visit
- Features about different aspects of the island that make it special
- Detailed listings of restaurants, hotels, shops and nightlife
- Practical information

In addition, easy-to-read side panels provide fascinating extra facts and snippets, highlights of places to visit and invaluable practical advice.

CROSS-REFERENCES

To help you make the most of your visit, cross-references, indicated by ▶, show you where to find additional information about a place or subject.

MAPS

The Top 25 locator maps found on the inside front and back covers of the book itself are for quick reference. They show the Top 25 Sights, described on pages 24–48, which are clearly plotted by number (**1**–**25**, not page number) in alphabetical order. The grid references given in this book refer to these maps.
The fold-out map in the wallet at the back of the book is a large-scale map of Menorca.

PRICES

Where appropriate, an indication of the cost of an establishment is given by € signs: €€€ denotes higher prices, €€ denotes average prices, while € denotes lower charges.

MENORCA
life

A Personal View *6–7*

Menorca in Figures *8*

People of Menorca *9*

A Chronology *10–11*

Best of Menorca *12*

Menorca Life

A Personal View

MAÓ AND CIUTADELLA

The rivalry between the two cities continues today, with both sides vulnerable to a certain superiority complex. The people of Maó consider themselves more intellectual; the people of Ciutadella are happy to agree, but only because they consider themselves more artistic. It was the Count of Cifuentes, the first Spanish governor following British rule, who captured the difference perfectly with a saying which many believe still holds true: 'Maó may have more people, but Ciutadella has more souls'.

The Molí dés Compte windmill, Ciutadella

Menorca is rather like a person who doesn't stand out in a crowd and is modest about their own achievements, but actually proves rather interesting once you get to know them. For too long Menorca has lived in the shadow of its Balearic neighbours, whose more marketable attractions have pushed it into third place in the Balearic tourist league. Mallorca may be bigger, Ibiza may be louder, but Menorca remains aloof, quietly confident of its own charms. The canny Menorcans know that there is more to life than tourism and, as a result, those who come here appreciate the island all the more.

Menorca has more beaches than Mallorca and Ibiza combined, but they are a little harder to find. To reach them, you might have to drive across farmland or hike along a forest track. The result is that not many people bother. Even in summer, there are plenty of remote beaches which are rarely crowded, and out of season you should be able to find a pine-fringed cove which you can have all to yourself.

Not that Menorca is all about beaches. The island has often been called an open-air historical museum. Ancient watchtowers and burial chambers dot the landscape, built by Bronze Age settlers and still standing undisturbed in the middle of fields. They are remnants of the Talaiotic culture, which thrived on Menorca from around 2000 BC. Later invaders have left their mark too. The Romans introduced Christianity, the Arabs brought horses (still a Menorcan passion) and the Aragonese conquest of 1287 introduced the Catalan language, which is still spoken today. Among the legacies of 18th-century British rule are the dairy industry, Georgian architecture and a predilection for gin among the inhabitants.

The cities at either end of the island, each no bigger than a small provincial town, make an intriguing contrast of styles. They may be just 45km apart but they face in different directions, as if deliberately turning their backs on one

Menorca Life

Cales Fonts is an attractive harbour not far from the main square in Es Castell

another. Maó, the Georgian colonial capital, is a busy place of civil servants and naval officers, looking outwards to the Mediterranean and protected by one of the world's great harbours. Ciutadella, on the other hand, faces Mallorca and Catalonia and has a much more Spanish feel, with a Gothic cathedral surrounded by the palaces of the Catalan nobility.

Between the two cities lies a bucolic rural landscape of meadows, cattle and drystone walls, punctuated by a handful of solid market towns strung out along the single main road. Dairy farming is still important here, along with a few small-scale industries producing shoes, cheese and ice cream. Tourism is important too, but it has not been at the expense of everything else – the Menorcans are determined not to repeat the mistakes from which Mallorca and Ibiza are only just starting to recover. Menorca's designation as a UNESCO Biosphere Reserve encourages traditional industries and tourism to work in partnership with conservation, ensuring that any change is carefully managed and sustainable. Somehow, you feel, the Menorcans have got their priorities right.

MADE IN MENORCA

Menorca and its capital have given their name to a number of popular foodstuffs. Queso de Mahón, manufactured in Alaior, is one of Spain's best-known cheeses; La Menorquina, also from Alaior, is its most popular brand of ice cream. Perhaps most interesting is mayonnaise, said to have been invented by the Duc de Richelieu's housekeeper during the French occupation of Maó (Mahón) and named *salsa mahonesa* after the city.

Menorca Life

Menorca in Figures

GEOGRAPHY AND LANDSCAPE

- Menorca is the second largest of the Balearic Islands, a group that includes Mallorca, Ibiza and Formentera.
- Menorca lies 225km southeast of Barcelona at the eastern extremity of Spain.
- Menorca measures 53km from east to west and 23km from north to south at its widest point.
- Menorca has 220km of coastline, with more beaches than all the other Balearic Islands put together.
- The highest mountain is Monte Toro (358m).
- Menorca has at least 1,000 prehistoric monuments and 15,000km of drystone walls.

CLIMATE

- Menorca has an average daily maximum temperature of 20°C, rising to 28°C in July and falling to 14°C in January, and an average of 315 sunny days a year.
- Menorca is the wettest of the Balearic Islands (the rainy season is October to April).

PEOPLE

- Menorca has a population of 75,000, of whom around 25,000 live in Maó and 25,000 in Ciutadella.

TOURISM

- In 1950 Menorca had 200 hotel rooms; by 1995 it had 40,000 rooms in hotels and apartments.
- Menorca received 8,000 tourists in 1960, 200,000 in 1980 and 1.1 million in 2000. In 2000, 58 per cent of visitors were from Britain, 15 per cent from Germany and 16 per cent from Spain.
- About 98 per cent of tourists arrive between April and October.

LANGUAGE

- Most people speak Menorquín, which is a dialect of Catalan. Since 1983 Catalan and Castilian Spanish have both been official languages, but there has been a revival of Catalan, especially in place names.
- Menorquín contains a number of words inherited during the 18th-century British occupation – examples include *grevi* (gravy) and *winder* (a sash window).

People of Menorca

Alfonso III of Aragón (1265–91)

Although he spent only 45 days on Menorca, the hero of the Reconquest can take most of the credit for the influence of Catalan culture on the island. Succeeding to the throne at the age of 20, he immediately set about planning to capture Menorca. He sailed from the mainland in 1286, reached Maó in January 1287 and conquered Menorca two weeks later. During his brief stay he established a system of government that was to last for several centuries; he also distributed land among his followers, earning the nickname 'the Liberal' since he rarely refused a request. He was capable of cruelty as well – those Moors too poor to pay a ransom and too weak to work as slaves were simply taken out to sea and drowned. Alfonso died in Barcelona at the age of 25; his statue, donated by General Franco, stands in the Plaça Conquesta in Maó.

Sir Richard Kane (1662–1736)

When the British arrived in Menorca, resistance to Protestant rule and resentment at the duplicitous nature of their conquest meant there was a need for a governor who would win Menorcans' respect. Richard Kane fitted the bill perfectly. A Northern Irish soldier who had served in Flanders and Canada, he arrived in 1713 to become Lieutenant-Governor. His first act was to build a road across the island, from Maó to Ciutadella, financed by a tax on alcohol – much of the road still stands. At the same time he moved the capital from Ciutadella to Maó. He drained marshes, planted orchards, introduced Friesian cattle, and made daily visits to the market in Maó to check on the prices and measures. Agricultural production increased by five times in 40 years. Kane remained in Menorca until his death and was buried in Fort Sant Felip. He is remembered on Menorca with affection, and a monument to his achievements stands near the start of the Camí d'en Kane (▶ 19).

MATEU ORFILA (1787–1853)

Dr Mateu Orfila was born in Menorca but became Dean of Medicine at the University of Paris. He is known as the founder of modern forensic medicine after his ground-breaking work on toxicology in 1813. A bust of Dr Orfila stands outside his house in Carrer Ses Moreres, Maó.

JOAN PONS

The baritone Joan Pons (1946–) was born in Ciutadella and still visits Menorca as often as time allows. Since 1980 he has performed at opera houses across Europe and North America, including La Scala in Milan, La Fenice in Venice, Covent Garden in London and the Metropolitan Opera in New York. In June 2001 he played Falstaff at the opening night of Maó's restored Teatre Principal.

This monument to the memory of Sir Richard Kane was erected by the Menorcan people in 1973

Menorca Life

A Chronology

About 100 million years ago	Fragments of continental Europe and Andalusia fuse, forming Menorca.
2,000–123 BC	The Talaiotic period produces burial caves, *navetas* and settlements with *talaiots* and *taulas* (➤ 21).
400 BC	Carthaginian invaders enlist Balearic slingshot throwers to fight in the Punic Wars; they are paid in wine and women.
123 BC	Roman conquest; Menorca is named Balearis Minor. Under Roman rule, Christianity is introduced, and towns are established at Maó, Ciutadella and Sanitja.
AD 533	After a century of Vandal rule, Menorca becomes part of the Byzantine Empire.
902	The Balearic Islands enter the Caliphate of Córdoba, under Islamic rule.
1229	Jaume I of Aragón conquers Mallorca. The Arab rulers agree to become his vassals, paying an annual tribute in wheat, cattle and lard.
1287	Alfonso III of Aragón lands at Maó – the Moors surrender and Christianity is restored. Alfonso dies in 1291 aged 25. Menorca is ruled by the kings of Mallorca and Catalan becomes the main language.
1349	Menorca is incorporated into Aragón.
1492	Aragón unites with Castile and Granada to create modern Spain.
1535	More than half the population of Maó are killed or enslaved by the Turkish pirate Barbarossa.
1554	Fort Sant Felip is constructed.
1558	Most of Ciutadella is destroyed by a Turkish raid.
17th century	The British gain treaty rights to the use of Port de Maó. Maó becomes the main city.

Menorca Life

1708	The British occupy Menorca in the name of Charles, Archduke of Austria.
1713	The Treaty of Utrecht confirms British rule.
1756	The Battle of Menorca ends in a French victory and the execution of the British Admiral Byng.
1763–82	British rule returns to Menorca, under the Treaty of Paris, and Georgetown (Es Castell) is built.
1782–98	Menorca returns to Spanish rule. Fort Sant Felip is destroyed. In 1798 the British retake Menorca without loss of life.
1802	The Treaty of Amiens returns Menorca to Spain.
1854	A steamer service from Maó to Barcelona opens.
1909	A Society for the Attraction of Foreigners is formed.
1936–39	The Spanish Civil War; Menorca is the last part of Spain to surrender to General Franco. Under Franco's dictatorship (1939–75), the use of the Catalan language is forbidden.
1953	The first charter flight from England lands.
1969	The opening of Sant Climent airport leads to the tourist boom.
1975	Franco dies and the monarchy is restored.
1983	The Balearic Islands become an autonomous region, with Catalan as an official language.
1986	Spain joins the European Community.
1993	Menorca is declared a UNESCO Biosphere Reserve.
2002	As visitor numbers reach 1 million, the Balearic government introduces an eco-tax on tourists.

Menorca Life

Best of Menorca

If you only have a short time to visit Menorca, and are looking for the best way to experience the essence of the island, here are some suggested activities and places to visit:

- Take a boat trip around Maó harbour (➤ 42), then stroll along the waterfront for a drink in Cala Figuera.
- Wander the back streets of Ciutadella, where every other house is the palace of a noble family, with hidden architectural details and coats of arms above the door (➤ 34–36).
- Have lunch by the harbour at Fornells (➤ 39) – try *caldereta de langosta* (➤ 68) if you can afford it.
- Walk to a remote beach inaccessible by car – take a picnic and remember to carry plenty of water.
- Seek out some of Menorca's prehistoric sites and try to unravel the mystery of the *taulas* (➤ 21).
- Go to the trotting races in Maó or Ciutadella at weekends (➤ 81), the best place to see Menorcans indulge their passion for horses.
- Find a festival (➤ 22) – the Festa de Sant Joan in Ciutadella is one of the best.
- Make a pilgrimage (on foot or by car) to the hilltop convent of Monte Toro (➤ 44).
- Try some Mahón cheese (➤ 74), then buy some to take home.
- Lie on the beach soaking up the sun – everyone does it at least once. But don't forget your sunblock.

The traffic-free streets in the centre of Maó are home to some of the smartest shops on Menorca

Sun, sea and sand – the Mediterranean dream

MENORCA
how to organise your time

WALKS & DRIVES *14–19*

A Walk Around Maó
A Drive from Ciutadella to Maó
A Walk from Es Castell
A Drive Around the Southeast
A Coastal Walk to Sa Torreta
A Drive Along the Camí d'en Kane

FINDING PEACE & QUIET *20–21*

WHAT'S ON *22*

How to Organise Your Time

A Walk Around Maó

INFORMATION

Distance 3km
Time 1 hour
Start/end point
Plaça de S'Esplanada
🚍 Buses from all over the island terminate here
Lunch
Mirador Café (€)
✉ Plaça de d'Espanya 2
☎ 971 35 21 07

Begin in Plaça de S'Esplanada (➤ 43) with your back to the barracks and take Carrer Ses Moreres in the right-hand corner. Head down this street, noting the bust of Dr Orfila (➤ 9) outside No. 13.

Continue into another shopping street, Carrer Hannóver, which drops sharply to Plaça Constitució. Turn right into Carrer Nou; this brings you to Plaça Reial. Turn left to reach Plaça del Carme. Cross this square diagonally to look into the cloistered market, then head down the steps to the fish market in Plaça d'Espanya.

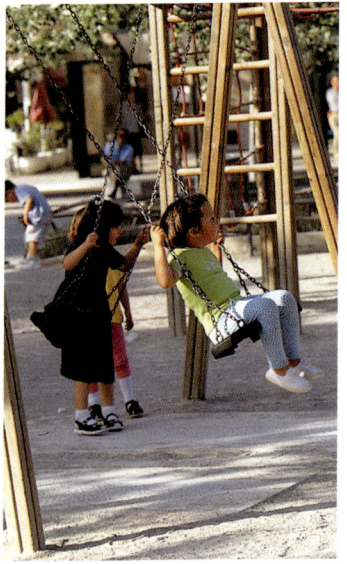

You could drop down to the waterfront here – but to continue your city walk, follow the stone railings around the square into Plaça Conquesta, with its statue of the Conqueror, Alfonso III. The narrow alley off the square to the right gives a splendid view of the harbour.

Leave Plaça Conquesta diagonally opposite where you entered to return to Plaça Constitució. Turn right by the town hall then bear left into Carrer Isabel II, whose Georgian houses back on to the harbour walls.

The road ends at the Museu de Menorca.

Plaça de S'Esplanada, where the walk begins and ends, is the best place to see the people of Maó at play

Turn left to enter a maze of narrow streets and whitewashed houses. Another left turn, then right, brings you to Carrer Sant Antoni, emerging beside an old convent, now an art gallery. Turn left to reach Pont de Sant Roc, the only remaining section of the city walls. Turn right into Plaça Bastió and cross this square to enter Carrer d'Alaior. Turn right at the end to return to Plaça de S'Esplanada.

How to Organise Your Time

A Drive from Ciutadella to Maó

The map of Menorca is dominated by one road, the Me-1 connecting Maó to Ciutadella. A drive along the length of this road passes three inland towns and several prehistoric sites.

Start on the edge of Ciutadella, at the roundabout which features a sculpture of a prancing horse. Pass the football stadium and the industrial estate on your left, with factory shops competing for your attention. After 4km the car park for Naveta des Tudons (➤ 45) is reached on the right; shortly after this there are more turn-offs to Torre Trencada and Torre Llafuda. After 9km, skirt a crest by Castillo Menorca, where you will have your first view of the central mountains.

INFORMATION

Distance 44km one way
Time 1 hour
Start point
Ciutadella
✚ A2
End point
Maó
✚ E3
Lunch
Molí des Racó (€€)
✉ Carrer Vicario Fuxà 53, Es Mercadal
☎ 971 37 53 92

After passing the manor house of Binisues on your left, a series of bends takes you up to Ferreries (➤ 38). The road continues to Es Mercadal (➤ 53), with Monte Toro (➤ 44) dominating the view.

Shortly after bypassing Es Mercadal, Camí d'en Kane (➤ 19) leads off to the left; next you climb a twisting hill to a picnic area overlooking the rock formation known as Sa Penya de S'Indio, because of its apparent resemblance to an Indian brave. From here the road bypasses Alaior (➤ 24), then goes fast and straight to Maó.

Keep straight ahead at the industrial estate, following signs for 'Centre Ciutat'. Bear right at the mini-roundabout to reach Plaça de S'Esplanada, the start of the walk around Maó (➤ 14).

Ferreries, Menorca's highest town

You can return to Ciutadella the same way, or combine this with one of the other drives (➤ 17 and 19). Alternatively, take the pretty country roads between Es Mercadal and Ferreries via Es Migjorn Gran (➤ 37).

How to Organise Your Time

A Walk from Es Castell

INFORMATION

Distance 10km
Time 2½ hours
Start/end point
Es Castell
🚍 F3
🚌 Bus from Maó
Lunch
Ca'n Delio (€€)
✉ Cales Fonts 38

Start the walk in Plaça de S'Esplanada, outside the town hall.

Facing the military museum, head right along Carrer Cales Fonts. Turn right into Miranda de Cala Corb and follow the promenade, dropping down to the harbour at Cala Corb and climbing the steps to Carrer Sant Cristòfol on the far side. At the end of this road turn left. Cross the roundabout and walk uphill. Turn left at the crossroads; just after passing Carrer des Fusters on the left, the road bends right.

Turn left when you come to the entrance to the *depuradora* (water treatment plant) onto a country lane that continues across farmland between walls, eventually arriving at a road.

Cross the road and take the track opposite; when this joins another road bear right. Passing a military base, turn left on to a wide track marked Horts de Binissaida. At the end of this track, go left on a walled path – when the wall on your right runs out, climb through a gap and follow the footpath towards the sea. Soon you drop down to Cala de Sant Esteve (▶ 51), arriving beside the entrance to the Marlborough.

The harbour at Cales Fonts is perfectly placed to catch the midday sun

Walk around the bay and climb the narrow path at the far end to rejoin the road. Turn right at the cemetery. This road skirts the Sol del Este estate before reaching a small cove. Drop down to the beach then climb up the other side; continue through a modern estate and over another road. Turn right at the T-junction to reach Cales Fonts for lunch; from here, Carrer Stuart leads back to the main square.

How to Organise Your Time

A Drive Around the Southeast

This drive takes in Menorca's only stretch of coast road.

Start in Maó, leaving Plaça de S'Esplanada on the airport road. Turn left at the first roundabout and left again at the next. Follow signs to Sant Lluís. Go straight through Sant Lluís (➤ 53) and over the roundabout towards the coast. After 1km, take the right fork to Punta Prima and after another 1km – when you see a huge satellite mast ahead – fork left, climbing a hill and dropping down to the sea. As you enter Punta Prima, a right turn at the first roundabout (Carrer de Llevant) takes you on to the coast road.

Follow this road for 5km until you see Binibeca Vell on your left. After exploring the village, a left turn at the next roundabout leads down to the sea and an idyllic lunch spot on the beach. When this road runs out, turn inland – go left at the T-junction, then swing a wide left at the three-way intersection to return to the coast.

Eventually the road leads inland across a rocky landscape, followed by gentle countryside on its way to Sant Climent.

Turn left through the village on to the Cala En Porter road; after 4km, just beyond the turn-off to Cales Coves, take the country road to Alaior on your right.

You cross a typical landscape of meadows and drystone walls, as well as passing some interesting prehistoric sites.

On reaching Alaior (➤ 24), turn right and return to Maó on the main road.

INFORMATION

Distance 48km
Time 2 hours plus lunch
Start/end point
Maó
✚ E3
Lunch
Los Bucaneros (€€)
✉ Binibèquer beach
🕒 May–Oct only

Stop off in Alaior to wander the narrow streets

How to Organise Your Time

A Coastal Walk to Sa Torreta

INFORMATION

Distance 11km
Time 3 hours plus picnic
Start/end point
Es Grau
F2
Buses from Maó in summer
Lunch
Take a picnic

This walk has everything – countryside, beaches, archaeology and coastal views. It crosses part of the S'Albufera reserve, a protected wetland.

Begin at the old-fashioned seaside village of Es Grau (► 46), walking around the beach to the far side opposite the car park. Climb the footpath on to the cliffs and turn right. The path rises and falls until you see Illa d'en Colom ahead. Follow the path down towards the sea, passing a cave house and crossing behind a small beach.

The path now swings left to cross a headland and drops to Fondeadero de los Llanes.

Walk around this bay, passing two inlets and a sandy beach, then up a slope on the far side. Climb over the wall to reach a sandy area and look for a narrow gap on the left leading to a cart track. Make a careful note of this spot – there is a red arrow on a stone to guide you – and turn left.

The walk from Es Grau leads along a wild section of the coast

An easy circular walk returns you to this same spot. The track skirts the S'Albufera lagoon then climbs to Sa Torreta farm after 30–40 minutes.

At the farm, an overgrown path beside a concrete barn leads to Sa Torreta. Leaving the farm, take the track straight ahead. The track descends to Cala de Sa Torreta, shaded by pine woods, then climbs above the bay, passing another beach before turning inland. Now look for the junction where you began the circular walk. Turn left to return to Es Grau by the same route.

At Es Grau beach, go through the gap between the dunes to cross part of the S'Albufera reserve. You emerge on the main road a few minutes south of the village.

How to Organise Your Time

A Drive Along the Camí d'en Kane

In 1713 the British built a new road from Maò to Ciutadella. Parts of the road still exist.

Start by the ferry station on the waterfront at Maó. Take the road north for Fornells. Shortly after leaving the harbour you pass a monument to Sir Richard Kane, the first British governor, on your right. After another 2km, turn left on to a quiet country road, the Camí d'en Kane.

This road rises and falls through typical Menorcan countryside. After 9km note the town of Alaior to your left and a cemetery on your right.

Keep straight ahead as the road narrows and passes beneath a canopy of pine trees.

Monte Toro rises up ahead of you – a recurring feature of the next few kilometres. Eventually Camí d'en Kane ends and you join the main highway from Maó to Ciutadella (from here it roughly follows the route of Kane's original road).

Turn right and almost immediately right again, skirting the town of Es Mercadal and following the signs to Fornells (► 39), a good spot for a harbourside lunch.

Leave Fornells by the same road; after 3km, turn left towards Maó.

This road passes through some of Menorca's most thickly wooded areas before returning to Maó harbour. Several roads to the left lead to various north coast resorts.

INFORMATION

Distance 56km
Time 1½ hours plus lunch
Start point
Maó harbour
✚ F3
End point
Maó
✚ E3
Lunch
S'Ancora (€€)
✉ Passeig Marítim 8, Fornells

The drive passes this boldly coloured façade

How to Organise Your Time

Finding Peace & Quiet

CAMÍ DE CAVALLS

This bridleway around the entire Menorcan coast was first built in the 14th century and restored during the brief French occupation of 1756–63. It has mostly fallen into disrepair; ambitious plans to reopen the whole route have met with opposition from landowners and to date only a small section in the southeast has been reconstructed.

It's not difficult to find peace and quiet in Menorca – sometimes it's harder to get away from it. Even on the most crowded beaches, you are never more than a short walk away from a peaceful cove, fragrant pine woods or tranquil countryside. Go in winter and you have the island to yourself; only one tourist in 100 arrives between November and March. You might have to wrap up against the north wind, but winter and, especially, early spring are beautiful on Menorca, and the mild sunny days are perfect for walking.

WALKING

The paths and minor roads that have criss-crossed Menorca since Roman times provide gentle walking on largely flat land. The biggest challenges are the hills of Monte Toro (➤ 44) and Santa Agueda (➤ 51), but even these can be managed by anyone who is reasonably fit. Other good areas are the limestone gorges of the south (➤ 25) and the numerous coastal paths. Walking in the countryside, you encounter an attractive rural landscape of Moorish farmhouses, curved olive-wood gates, sheep-shelters and drystone walls. Rights of way are not always clear and forbidding notices are not uncommon, but a word with the farmer will often help. Remember to shut all gates and not to walk over crops. Wherever you are walking, it is a good idea to carry water and food and to protect yourself from the sun.

The Roman road to the summit of Santa Agueda gives spectacular views across the island

PREHISTORIC SITES

Menorca's prehistoric sites are among the most peaceful places on the island. Most are situated in the midst of farmland; although they are on private land visitors have free, open access to all but a handful of sites.

The most common monuments include *navetas*, burial chambers shaped like an upturned boat, and *talaiots*, large circular structures used as both dwellings and watchtowers. Most mysterious of all are the *taulas*, T-shaped 'tables' which probably performed some religious ritual function.

BIRDS AND FLOWERS

Menorca is a popular staging-post for thousands of migrant birds each spring and autumn, pausing for rest on their way across the Mediterranean. The best sites for birdwatching are the S'Albufera marshes (▶ 46), the southern gorges and the wilder coastal areas. Endemic species include red kites and booted eagles, as well as the brightly coloured bee-eater, which nests in sandbanks and dunes. The cliffs, fields, gorges and woods of Menorca become a riot of wild flowers in spring; among more than 200 species are several varieties of orchid, which come into flower between March and May.

The Algendar Gorge is a haven for insect life

Spring flowers and wildlife in the Algendar Gorge

How to Organise Your Time

What's On

JANUARY	*Los Reyes Magos* (5 Jan): The Three Kings arrive by boat in Maó to deliver Christmas presents to the city's children the next day. *Sant Antoni Abad* (16–17 Jan): Bonfires, dancing and fancy dress parties in Maó, Es Castell and elsewhere on 16 Jan; on 17 Jan, after Mass in Ciutadella cathedral, there is a horseback procession to Plaça Alfons III.
MARCH/APRIL	*Setmana Santa* (Holy Week): Palm branches are blessed on Palm Sunday, then taken home to adorn balconies and doors. Processions take place in Maó and Ciutadella on Good Friday.
JUNE	*Sant Joan* (23–24 Jun): Menorca's most colourful festival, with traditions dating back to the Middle Ages. There is a horseback procession around Plaça des Born in Ciutadella on the evening of 23 June, with further processions on 24 June, as well as Mass in the cathedral, jousting and fireworks. The celebrations begin the Sunday before 24 June (the Day of the Sheep), when a live lamb is carried around town by a man dressed in sheepskins.
JULY	*Festa Patriòtica* (9 Jul): Ciutadella commemorates resistance against Turkish attack in 1558. *La Verge del Carme* (16 Jul): Processions of fishing boats in Maó, Ciutadella and Fornells in honour of the protector of fishermen. *Sant Martí* (3rd weekend): Processions of horses, giants and Carnival figures in Es Mercadal. *Sant Jaume* (24–26 Jul): Horseback parades and merriment in Es Castell. *Sant Antoni* (4th weekend): Festivities in Fornells include *jaleo* dancing on the waterfront.
AUGUST	*Sant Cristòfol* (early Aug): Es Migjorn Gran; includes 'blessing of vehicles' by parish priest. *Sant Llorenç* (Sun after 10 Aug): *Caragols* dancing and prancing in the streets of Alaior. *Sant Bartomeu* (23–25 Aug): Frolics in Ferreries, with cavalcades, music and dancing. *Sant Lluís* (last weekend): Parades, parties and firework displays.
SEPTEMBER	*La Verge del Gràcia* (7–9 Sep): Maó's main festival. Cavalcades, street parties, donkey races, fireworks and regattas in the harbour.
DECEMBER	*Nadal* (Christmas, 24–25 Dec): Midnight Mass in churches across Menorca.

MENORCA's
top 25 sights

The sights are shown on the maps on the inside front cover and inside back cover, numbered **1**–**25** alphabetically

1. Alaior *24*
2. Barranc d'Algendar (Algendar Gorge) *25*
3. Binibeca Vell *26*
4. Cala d'Algaiarens *27*
5. Cala En Turqueta *28*
6. Cala Macarella *29*
7. Cala Morell *30*
8. Cala Pregonda *31*
9. Cala Santa Galdana *32*
10. Cales Coves *33*
11. Ciutadella *34*
12. Ciutadella's Museu Municipal *35*
13. Ciutadella's Plaça des Born *36*
14. Es Migjorn Gran *37*
15. Ferreries *38*
16. Fornells *39*
17. Maó *40*
18. Maó's Església del Carme *41*
19. Maó Harbour *42*
20. Maó's Plaça de S'Esplanada *43*
21. Monte Toro *44*
22. Naveta des Tudons *45*
23. S'Albufera des Grau *46*
24. Son Bou *47*
25. Torre d'en Galmés *48*

23

Top **25**

1

Alaior

INFORMATION

- D3
- Bars and cafés; The Cobblers restaurant (€€)
- Buses from Maó and Ciutadella
- Market Mon, Thu. *Festa de Sant Llorenç*, Sun following 10 Aug

Say cheese – especially if you're in Alaior

An ancient town of narrow streets and whitewashed houses, Alaior is also famous for cheese-making.

Menorca's third largest town, 12km west of Maó, was founded by Jaume II of Mallorca in 1304 when he divided the island into seven regions, each with a central market town. The existence of Roman roads around the town, and the wealth of prehistoric remains near by, suggest that it was a centre of population in much earlier times.

There are few specific sights in Alaior, but it makes a pleasant place to stroll – a town of gleaming white houses huddled together in narrow streets which lead up to the parish church of Santa Eulàlia at the town's summit. Jaume II built the first church here; it was later fortified by villagers following the Turkish attacks on Maó and Ciutadella. The present baroque church dates from the 17th century.

Another 17th-century church, Sant Diego, was once a Franciscan convent – its peaceful cloisters have been turned into modern flats, set around a courtyard with an old well at its centre. You can enter the cloisters via a vaulted, whitewashed alley beside the church. The style is said to be based on the Spanish colonial missions in Mexico and California. The courtyard, now known as Sa Lluna, is the setting for concerts and folk dancing in summer.

Alaior is an important centre for the manufacture of shoes, ice cream and especially Mahón cheese (▶ 74). You can buy cheese at the Coinga factory shop, which is signposted as you enter the town from the south. The shop sells the full range from *fresco* (fresh and soft) to *añejo* (matured for two years and as strong as Parmesan), as well as various cheesy souvenirs and jars of cheese in olive oil.

Top **25**

2

Barranc d'Algendar (Algendar Gorge)

A dramatic limestone gorge, buzzing with wildlife, which runs for 6km from Ferreries to the south coast.

Menorca's *barrancs*, or gorges, are wild and lonely places, deep clefts formed over tens of thousands of years by the gradual erosion of the limestone plateau in the south.

The gorges attract a huge variety of wildlife – birds, butterflies and flowers. Kestrels and kites nestle among the rushes; you may well see herons, buzzards and booted eagles. Lizards sun themselves on the rocks and tortoises wade through the marshes. The combination of rainfall, humidity and protection from the wind produces a richness of vegetation rarely seen elsewhere on the island.

Algendar Gorge is the most dramatic of all – and one of the most challenging to explore. The stream flows throughout the year, opening out at Cala Santa Galdana (►32) into a wide river beside the beach. From here you can walk part of the way along its western side, where pine trees grow out of the cliffs at remarkable angles, but the path is often overgrown.

There is a greater sense of peace at the northern end. Take the minor road off the Maó–Ciutadella highway 100m west of the Cala Santa Galdana exit; when the tarmac runs out (beside a signed footpath to Ferreries on the old Camí Reial) turn down the lane to your right. You can walk a short way along the gorge before finding your path blocked.

INFORMATION

- C2
- At Cala Santa Galdana (€–€€)
- Buses from Maó, Ciutadella and Ferreries to Cala Santa Galdana in summer
- Cala Santa Galdana (►32)

The path through the Algendar Gorge leads past limestone outcrops

25

Top **25**

3

Binibeca Vell

INFORMATION

- E4
- Several bars and restaurants (€€)
- Buses from Maó in summer

An artful copy of a small Mediterranean town, Binibeca Vell betrays its secrets with a steeple that has no church, and a name that translates as 'Fishing Village'.

You'll either love or hate this place – it is difficult to feel anything in between. To some it is an example of tasteful tourist development, based on architectural beauty and local style; to others it is tacky, artificial and ugly. One of the earliest coastal developments in Menorca, it was designed to resemble a Mediterranean fishing village, with whitewashed houses, orange trees and sun-drenched patios filled with geraniums. A maze of narrow alleys, Moorish archways, boats and sea views, it would be stunning if only it were authentic. The first giveaway is the name – would a real fishing village be called *Poblat de Pescadors* ('Fishing Village')? Then there are the notices for 'reception' and 'public relations', and the signs asking people to be quiet. Look beneath the steeple for the village church and you find an alcove with a crucifix inside – the architect needed a church for the postcards but the temporary 'villagers' have no need of a real one.

You could spend your whole holiday here – there is a supermarket, souvenir shops, restaurants and bars, swimming pools, squash courts, a children's play area and a car hire office. The nearest beach is 1km away at Binibèquer – here you can hire sunshades, loungers and pedal boats and have lunch at a wooden shack which claims to be the only place in Menorca where you can have a drink with your feet in the sea.

A new coat of whitewash for Binibeca Vell (above)

Top **25**

4

Cala d'Algaiarens

A pair of beautiful beaches reached by a drive across private land, then a woodland walk – here is a peaceful location making no concessions to tourism.

These twin beaches on Menorca's remote northwest coast are reached by crossing the fertile La Vall region until you reach a pair of gateposts surmounted by offputting 'private' signs. In winter you are within your rights to drive on; in summer the landowner levies a toll, justified by the need to restrict traffic pollution.

Once through the gates, follow signs to '*playa*' and when the track runs out, walk through the woods – a haven for migrant bee-eaters in spring and summer – to reach the sea. The main beach is a wide horseshoe of golden sand backed by dunes – you can scramble over the low rocks to reach a second beach, Platja d'es Tancats. Both beaches shelve gently into the sea and offer safe bathing in sheltered waters. This is a lovely, peaceful spot which only really gets busy at summer weekends. There are no facilities.

INFORMATION

- B2
- None
- Cala Morell (▶ 30)

Walking along the tree-shaded pathway to the twin beaches

Top **25**

5

Cala En Turqueta

INFORMATION

- B3
- None
- Boat trips from Cala En Bosc and Ciutadella in summer

For those prepared to do without tourist facilities, Cala En Turqueta is a blissfully unspoilt beach, free from crowds and shaded by trees.

This beautiful spot could easily be destroyed by thoughtless development; as it is, it remains idyllic. The reason, as with so many of Menorca's beaches, is that it cannot be reached by road. Following a government campaign to reclaim the island's beaches there is now a bumpy track leading to a free car park behind the beach but this still feels like a place apart. Pine-covered cliffs look down on to clear blue water and a beach of soft white sand backs on to extensive pine woods. The beach itself shelves gently into the sea. For the best views, climb on to the western cliffs – the path here continues to the next cove, Cala des Talaier, and from there to Arenal de Son Saura (▶ 50).

Head for Cala En Turqueta to escape the crowds – although even here you will not be entirely alone

Top **25**

6

Cala Macarella

It's worth the long walk to this lovely cove, which many people consider one of the most perfect spots on Menorca's coast.

A hike of around 30 minutes from the west end of Cala Santa Galdana (➤ 32) across a fragrant headland covered with wild flowers and herbs ends in a wooden stairway leading down to this delightful cove where a *barranc* flows into the sea. It's a good way to escape the crowds in high summer but you won't be alone – there is a beach bar and even a rough road from Ciutadella that goes most of the way to the beach (it is a 20-minute walk from the car park). Pine trees reach almost to the water's edge, providing welcome shade, and the beach shelves gently into the sea, creating good conditions for swimming. Many people consider this one of the most perfect spots on the Menorcan coast.

Overlooking the bay on its western side are three large caves, once used as burial caves but now in service as holiday homes in summer. If you want more privacy, you can cross the headland above the caves to the even more perfect adjacent cove of Cala Macarelleta, where pine-fringed rocks surround a small sandy beach, popular with nudists. From the path on top of the headland you can look down on both coves at once, one of the best views anywhere on Menorca. The more adventurous can travel from one cove to the other by swimming. Cala Macarella and Cala Macarelleta both offer good anchorage for yachts.

INFORMATION

- B3
- Cafeteria Susy (€)
- Buses from Ferreries, Maó and Ciutadella to Cala Santa Galdana in summer
- Cala Santa Galdana (➤ 32)

The footpath from Cala Santa Galdana to Cala Macarella and Cala Macarelleta

29

Top **25**

7

Cala Morell

INFORMATION

+ B2
- Bars and restaurants (€€)
- Cala d'Algaiarens (➤ 27)

The caves of Cala Morell give you the chance to picture what life might have been like for Menorca's prehistoric inhabitants.

Eight kilometres from Ciutadella on Menorca's otherwise deserted northeast coast, Cala Morell is best known for its remarkable collection of prehistoric caves. Dating from the late Bronze and early Iron Ages, and used both as burial caves and as dwellings, they feature circular chambers with central pillars plus windows, chimneys and raised sleeping areas. Some even have elaborately carved motifs on their façades. It is easy to gain access to most of the caves; if your appetite is whetted, finds from these caves are on display at the delightful Museu de Menorca in Maó (➤ 55) and the Museu Municipal in Ciutadella (➤ 35).

There is a small beach at Cala Morell, reached by steps from the car parks at either end of the village, and there is good swimming and snorkelling from the rock platforms at the foot of the cliffs.

The *urbanización* above the beach, a collection of Ibizan-style whitewashed villas, is one of the most exclusive in Menorca. As you wander around the prehistoric caves, you cannot help wondering whether tourists in 3,000 years' time will be clambering over the ruins of these villas and speculating on what life was like for people in the 20th and 21st centuries.

Cala Morell, where you can play at being a caveman

Top **25**

8

Cala Pregonda

Cala Pregonda is a peaceful bay, backed by pine and tamarisk woods, in a remote and sheltered corner of the north coast.

INFORMATION

- C2
- None

Everyone has their own favourite Menorcan cove but the one factor they all have in common is that you cannot reach them by road. Approaching Cala Pregonda on foot, you wonder what all the fuss is about – surely a perfect cove cannot have concrete houses behind the beach? But sit against the dunes with your back to the houses, surrounded by wild flowers on a quiet day in spring or autumn, looking out beyond the shore to the sandstone rocks and beyond that to Cap de Cavallería (➤ 51), and you will soon feel the magic of this place.

An old Roman road runs from Santa Agueda (➤ 51), but the easiest approach is from Binimel-là. Take the steps over the wall at the west end of Binimel-là beach, follow the track for 10 minutes across salt flats and a pebbly cove, climb a small headland above the dunes, then drop down to the beach.

The water is crystal-clear, ideal for swimming, though you might have to navigate your way around yachts. A short distance out to sea is a rocky islet with its own sandy beach, just right for a couple of families. Near here is Es Prego, the sandstone outcrop said to resemble a hooded monk (*prego* means proclamation), carved into shape by the fierce north wind. And behind the beach are the pine woods, the best place to take a picnic if you want to escape the crowds – and the sun.

And the houses? They were put up before the restrictions on coastal development were introduced. Even such modest building would not be allowed now.

The first sight of Cala Pregonda as you approach on foot from Binimel-là

Top **25**

9

Cala Santa Galdana

INFORMATION

- B3
- Wide choice of restaurants
- Buses from Ferreries, Maó and Ciutadella in summer
- Barranc d'Algendar (➤ 25), Cala Macarella (➤ 29), Cala Mitjana (➤ 50)

Cala Santa Galdana is a popular holiday destination, combining excellent facilities with an idyllic setting

Cala Santa Galdana is the 'queen of the coves', and enthusiastic tourist development reflects its popularity; however, it is also a site of scientific importance due to the rare flora and fauna that flourish in the mild climate.

One of Menorca's most beautiful (and ecologically important) coves is also one of the most developed – as such it has become a focus for debate about the extent of *urbanización* on the island. Thirty years ago there was not even a road here; now there are three enormous hotels and dozens of restaurants and bars.

The 'queen of the coves' takes its name from the Arab word for the local river; there is in fact no saint Galdana. A wide arc of golden sand, bounded by wooded cliffs and an emerald sea, Cala Santa Galdana enjoys a unique microclimate with higher temperatures and lower winds than the surrounding *calas*. The Barranc d'Algendar (➤ 25) flows into the sea here, its mouth widened to form a marina for small boats. A footbridge across the stream leads to a rocky outcrop, almost an island, and a spectacularly sited bar-restaurant where you dine on a terrace directly overlooking the sea. For the best views of the entire bay, follow the signs to Mirador de Sa Punta on the eastern cliffs. You can also climb up here from the eastern end of the beach.

This is a good place to go in mid-season as a base for walks along the gorge or to some of the quieter beaches in both directions along the coast. In high season it is perfect for family holidays – fun and facilities for the children, safe swimming, and good shady walks for the adults. You can hire windsurfing and snorkelling equipment, pedaloes and motorboats, learn to sail or scuba-dive, or take a boat ride along the coast for a picnic at a peaceful cove.

Top **25**

10

Cales Coves

A sheltered harbour of turquoise water is surrounded by cliffs hollowed out by Bronze Age cave dwellers to provide homes for the living and resting places for the dead; some of the caves are still occupied intermittently today.

INFORMATION

- D3
- None
- Buses from Maó and Cala En Porter to Son Vitamina in summer

It takes an effort to get there – a rough four-wheel-drive track or a brisk 45-minute walk through the olive trees from Son Vitamina – but when you arrive at Cales Coves you are greeted by one of the most memorable sights on Menorca. The cliffs looking down on to this sheltered bay are home to more than 100 Bronze Age caves, carved out of the rock and used as both burial chambers and dwellings, with the living and the dead housed side by side. The oldest caves, seen on the left as you arrive, date back to the 9th century BC; follow the footpath over the rocks on your right to reach a second cove, passing more modern caves (4th century BC) whose features include windows, patios and interior cubicles. Some of these have Roman inscriptions, indicating that they continued to be occupied after the Talaiotic period. In recent years, a number of the caves have been illegally inhabited by squatters and latter-day troglodytes. After several unsuccessful attempts to evict them, the authorities barred access to the caves in 2001. Unfortunately this means that it is not usually possible to see inside, though there are plans to reopen the caves to the public in the future.

The prehistoric villagers chose a good site – the angle of the coves means they are hidden from the open sea. This also provides safe mooring for pleasure boats in summer. The beaches are pebbly rather than sandy, but there is good swimming from the rocks.

Remarkable carvings in the rock face at Cales Coves

Top **25**

11

Ciutadella

INFORMATION

- A2
- Plaça de la Catedral 5
- ☎ 971 38 26 93
- Wide range of cafés and restaurants in city centre (£–£££)

The pedestrian walkway of Ses Voltes, in Ciutadella's Old Town

The Count of Cifuentes, who was Governor of Menorca in the late 18th century, once said of this city: 'Maó may have more people, but Ciutadella has more souls'. A visit here will make clear the reason for his words.

Where Maó is bureaucratic, Ciutadella is artistic; where Maó has power, Ciutadella has style. The nobility and the church stayed behind when the capital was moved to Maó, with the result that Ciutadella remains a pure Catalan city, undiluted by British or French architecture or by the ideas that colonial rulers brought in their wake.

There were Carthaginian and Roman settlements here, and the Arabs made it their capital, but Ciutadella, Menorca's second town, reached its zenith in the 17th century, when the island's richest families settled here.

Wander the maze of narrow streets fanning out from the cathedral, their Gothic palaces each marked by a coat of arms carved above the door; sit beneath the palm trees in the Plaça des Born at dusk; join the citizens of Ciutadella for their annual festival, when richly caparisoned horses prance through the streets, and you begin to appreciate the truth of the Count of Cifuentes' *bon mot*.

Top **25**

12

Ciutadella's Museu Municipal

The building which now houses Ciutadella's Municipal Museum has been a granary, a factory and a store for water. Today it is home to a well-organised series of displays outlining the history of Menorca.

The Bastió de Sa Font was built as a fortress in the late 17th century; it was subsequently used as a grain store, a gas factory and a water tank before being fully renovated and opened as the city's museum in 1995. The displays, neatly laid out in a long, bright, vaulted gallery, are carefully captioned and there are leaflets available in English to help you to find your way around.

The museum tells the history of Menorca from pre-Talaiotic to Muslim times through a collection of fascinating exhibits gathered from archaeological excavations around the island – bone knives which go back 3,000 years, ancient spears and slingshots, Roman coins, jewellery, oil lamps and dice. The most gruesome display case contains a collection of Iron Age skulls, which show that the Talaiotic culture had developed advanced techniques in cranial pathology. As well as head wounds caused by blows from weapons, there are fractures resulting from trepanning, or surgery. Signs of scarring show that the patient survived the primitive operation and made a full recovery.

INFORMATION

- A2
- Bastió de Sa Font
- 971 38 02 97
- Tue–Sat 10–2 (summer 10–2, 6–9)
- In city centre (£–££)
- Inexpensive (free Wed)

3,000 years of Menorcan history can be traced at the Municipal Museum

Top **25**

13

Ciutadella's Plaça des Born

INFORMATION

- A2
- Wide choice of bars and restaurants (€–€€)
- Buses from west coast resorts to Plaça de S'Esplanada in summer; buses from Maó arrive 5 minutes' walk away
- Ciutadella (➤ 34)
- *Festa de Sant Joan*, 23–24 Jun (➤ 22)

Open-air cafés and elegant 19th-century buildings characterise one of the finest city squares in Spain.

During the Fascist era this square at the heart of Ciutadella was renamed after General Franco, but everyone continued to call it 'es Born'. The word *born* means parade-ground – the square was used for jousting contests in earlier times and is still the venue for an equestrian parade during the city's annual festivities in June.

At the centre of the square is an obelisk commemorating those citizens of Ciutadella who were killed or abducted into slavery during the Turkish raid of 1558. Much of Ciutadella was destroyed, including the *alcázar* or governor's palace. The crenellated town hall, with its Moorish-looking row of palms standing guard, was built in the 19th century on the same site. Peep inside to see the panelled ceilings, portraits of local worthies and the Gothic chamber on the first floor.

Across the square are two 19th-century palaces, those of the Torre-Saura and Salord families, built symmetrically to either side of Carrer Major del Born. Their neo-classical façades are dominated by Italianate loggias; the ground floors facing the square are given over to gift shops and cafés. Near by is the 19th-century theatre, and the adjoining coffee-house, Cercle Artistìc, with harbour views.

The graceful façades of 19th-century buildings in tree-fringed Plaça des Born

Top **25**

14

Es Migjorn Gran

This town, near the vast, atmospheric Cova des Coloms, is named after the geological formation of the area.

The name of this quiet place means 'the large town in the south', *es migjorn* being the local term for the low limestone plateau, broken by gorges, which dominates the landscape of southern Menorca. For 200 years the town was known as San Cristóbal, after a blacksmith who founded a township here in 1769 – but before that it was known locally as Es Migjorn Gran and it has recently reverted to its old name.

This is the only one of the inland towns not on the Maó–Ciutadella highway and it retains a certain provincial charm.

A short drive from Es Migjorn Gran is the Cova des Coloms – a dank, dark cave the size of a cathedral and buzzing with birds and bats. Follow signs from the Sant Tomàs end of town. Park in the car park, walk past the cemetery and along a wide track to the farm of Binigaus Vell, then look for a track on your left at another *cuevas* sign and stay on this path for about 30 minutes.

INFORMATION

- C2
- Bars and restaurants (€–€€)
- Buses from Maó and Ferreries, and a link to Sant Tomàs in summer
- Sant Agustí Vell (➤ 58)
- Market Wed. *Festa de Sant Cristòfol* late Jul/early Aug

The parish church of Sant Cristòfol in Es Migjorn Gran

Top **25**

15

Ferreries

INFORMATION

- C2
- Plenty of restaurants and bars (€–€€)
- Buses from Maó and Ciutadella
- Market Tue, Fri. *Festa de Sant Bartomeu* 23–25 Aug

Museu de la Natura
- Carrer Mallorca 2
- 971 37 45 05
- Tue–Sat 10–1, 5.30–8.30, Sun 10–1
- Inexpensive

A statue in a niche in the whitewashed façade of Ferreries church

Menorca's highest town is a centre for shoe manufacture and is also a good starting point for walks to view the spectacular limestone gorges.

The highest town in Menorca – 150m above sea level – was built in the shadow of the island's second-highest mountain, S'Enclusa. The name of the mountain means 'anvil' and it is thought that the town's name derives from the word for 'blacksmith' – this was probably a centre of smithing along the road from Maó to Ciutadella. The main industries nowadays are furniture and shoe manufacture; there are two factory shops selling high-class leather shoes.

Plaça d'Espanya, at the heart of the town, is a large modern square with a fountain and a children's play area. East and south of here are the wide avenues of the new town, which has expanded greatly since the 1940s; west and north are the narrow streets of a typical Menorcan town, all white houses with green shutters and a 19th-century parish church, Sant Bartomeu, adorned with simple white and cream arches. The town is overlooked from the main road by a fine stairway of cultivated terraces.

Less pretty than its neighbours Es Mercadal and Es Migjorn Gran, Ferreries nevertheless retains an honest, lived-in feel – perhaps because the successful local industries mean it is well-populated throughout the year. It is also becoming a centre for rural tourism; the Museu de la Natura, which opened in 1998, focuses on environmental themes.

Just outside Ferreries is Son Mercer de Baix, an early Talaiotic village overlooking the confluence of two gorges.

Top **25**

16

Fornells

Fornells is an attractive fishing village of low, whitewashed houses at the edge of a long, sheltered bay. King Juan Carlos of Spain is a regular visitor.

Fornells is everybody's idea of a Mediterranean fishing village – white-painted houses around a harbour bobbing with boats, restaurants on the waterfront along a palm-lined promenade. Tourism is now more important than fishing, but there is still an industry here and the fish in the restaurants is genuinely local and fresh. Fornells is famous for its spiny lobsters, the essential ingredient in a *caldereta de langosta* (➤ 68). King Juan Carlos of Spain sails over regularly from Mallorca just to eat lobster at Fornells.

The village is built on the west side of the Bay of Fornells. The natural harbour is 5km long, similar to Maó's but shallower. The commander of the first British invasion force told his superiors that Maó and Fornells were the best ports in the Mediterranean.

Founded to defend the north coast against pirate ships, Fornells grew in importance in the 17th century with the building of Castell Sant Antoni. The castle ruins stand beside the sea, facing a small island crowned by a watchtower. A promenade from here, by the water's edge, leads to the cape, where there is a lighthouse, a small rock shrine and another watchtower, Torre de Fornells, opened as a museum. You can climb to the top of the tower to experience what would once have been the view of approaching invaders.

But most visitors don't go to Fornells for history. They go to soak up its simple beauty, to walk beside the quay then choose a harbourside restaurant to enjoy the freshest fish possible.

INFORMATION

- D2
- Wide choice of restaurants on the quayside (€€–€€€)
- Buses from Maó
- *Festa de la Verge del Carme* – procession and blessing of boats, 16 Jul. *Festa de Sant Antoni* – patronal festival, fourth weekend in Jul

Torre de Fornells
- Tue–Sat 11–2, 5–8; Sun 11–2
- Moderate (free Sun)

The picturesque fishing village of Fornells

Top **25**

17

Maó

INFORMATION

- E3
- Wide range of cafés and restaurants (€–€€€)
- Maó's main festival is *La Verge del Gràcia* in Sep; includes fireworks displays, street parties and a regatta
- Sa Rovellada de Dalt 24
  ☎ 971 36 37 90
  🕒 Mon–Fri 9–1, 3–7; Sat 9–1

A bas-relief of the British coat of arms in the stairwell of Maó's town hall

There was a city here in Roman times; its name, Magón, is probably derived from a Phoenician word meaning 'shelter'.

You cannot separate Maó from its harbour – without it, the city would not be there. The harbour is the reason why the great powers fought over Menorca for so long; it is the reason why the British moved the capital to Maó in 1722. The best way to arrive in Maó is by boat, sailing into the harbour past its various islands and watching as the city appears, 25m up on the cliff face, a jumble of attractive white-washed houses which seem to grow out of the old sea walls. Ferries from Barcelona, cruise ships and naval vessels, luxury yachts and even the odd fishing boat share space in the deep, clear waters and the narrow waterfront road is lined with restaurants and bars.

The British have had a considerable influence on today's city. It was they who filled it with Georgian-style architecture not seen anywhere else in Spain. Streets such as Carrer Isabel II are adorned with grand 18th-century houses, with furniture in the style of Sheraton and Chippendale and bow windows leaning across the pavement.

For three centuries Maó (frequently still referred to by its Spanish name, *Mahón*) had to serve its foreign rulers, whether British, French or Spanish. The result is a city that is serious rather than stylish, industrious rather than flamboyant. At times its status as a capital makes it feel like a much bigger city; at other times, when work is done for the day and everyone greets everyone else by name during the evening *passeig* across the Plaça de S'Esplanada, it feels like little more than a village.

Top **25**

18

Maó's Església del Carme

This formidable church was built in the 18th century but has since been much restored. Maó's main market shelters in its cloisters.

This massive baroque church was built in 1751 as a Carmelite convent but extensive damage during the Spanish Civil War means that most of what you see is heavily restored. The stern façade leads to a bright interior with bare stone walls and arches and a vaulted ceiling. During the original building of the church, a Roman necropolis was discovered in the vaults, along with various coins and urns which are now in the Museu de Menorca (➤ 55). Next to the church, the cloisters of the convent have been turned into a covered shopping mall that incorporates Maó's main market, as well as a supermarket in the basement. This is a good place to buy Mahón cheese, as well as cured hams and local sausages.

INFORMATION

- E3
- Plaça del Carme
- 971 36 24 02
- Near by (€–€€)
- Free
- The Collecció Hernández Mora, a small museum displaying Menorcan furniture, books and maps, is in the church cloisters.
- Folk dancing displays are held in the shopping mall on Thursday evenings in summer

The bare stone walls of Església del Carme were designed to make the church harder to attack

Top **25**

19

Maó Harbour

INFORMATION

- F3
- Waterfront restaurants at Maó and Es Castell (€€–€€€)
- Buses between Maó and Es Castell
- Boat tours of the harbour from Maó and Es Castell in summer
- Maó (➤ 40), Es Castell (➤ 53), Fort Sant Felip (➤ 52)

This deep, natural harbour is the glory of Maó – it has protected Menorca's capital throughout its history.

When the European powers fought over Menorca in the 18th century, the greatest prize was the harbour at Maó. The world's second largest natural harbour, 5km long and up to 900m wide, was wrongly believed to provide an impregnable Mediterranean base.

The best way to see the harbour is on one of the boat tours that leave from the foot of the harbour steps in summer. The water is deep but it remains incredibly clear, and from a glass-bottomed boat you can see the sea bed. From the water you get the best views of the 18th-century houses lining either side. High on a cliff between Maó and Es Castell is the Hotel del Almirante, a plum-red Georgian villa which was the home of the British Admiral Collingwood, Lord Nelson's second in command. Facing it on the north shore is Sant Antoni (Golden Farm), where Nelson is said to have stayed in 1799.

Between Maó and the harbour entrance are three islands. The first, Illa del Rei (King's Island), was the first place to be 'liberated' by Alfonso III; when the British built a hospital here, it was known as 'Bloody Island'. Next comes Illa Plana (Flat Island), a former quarantine island; this function was taken over in 1900 by the largest island, Lazareto, whose high walls were designed to prevent infections from reaching Maó. South of Lazareto, at the entrance to the harbour, are the ruins of Fort Sant Felip (➤ 52); to the north is the headland of La Mola, the most easterly point in Spain.

The houses of Maó seem to grow out of the harbour walls

Top **25**

20

Maó's Plaça de S'Esplanada

A centre of city life, this square is filled with the buzz of conversation during the day as well as in the evenings.

This esplanade – the square between the barracks and the streets of the old town – is the best place to go to see the people of Maó at play. There are pigeons and palm trees, fountains and flower beds, a bowling alley and a children's playground, which is busy from late afternoon until dusk. Old men sit in the shade reading newspapers; teenagers queue for popcorn and ice cream.

On Tuesdays and Saturdays there is an open-air clothes market here; on Sundays, street entertainers join the crowds. During Maó's festivals Plaça de S'Esplanada acts as an outdoor venue for concerts and parties. The square is lined with cafés – a good place to come during the evening *passeig* to sit with a drink, feeling the pulse of Maó.

INFORMATION

- E3
- Lots of restaurants and cafés (€–€€)
- Buses to Maó from across the island terminate here
- Market Tue, Sat

Maó's residents come to the Plaça to watch the world go by

Top **25**

21

Monte Toro

INFORMATION

- D2
- 971 37 50 60
- Daily 7AM–8PM (6PM winter)
- Sa Posada (€€) and café (€)
- Free
- Es Mercadal (➤ 53)
- First Sun in May – blessing of the fields

A large statue of Christ welcomes weary pilgrims arriving at the summit of Monte Toro

The spiritual and physical high point of Menorca – a hilltop convent right at the centre of the island.

Menorca's highest mountain (358m) is crowned by a convent which has become an important centre of pilgrimage. Its name almost certainly derives from *al-tor*, Arabic for 'highest mountain', despite the local legend about a bull (*toro* in Spanish) who discovered a statue of the Virgin in a cleft in the rock.

Get there by driving or walking the twisting 3km road from Es Mercadal; an alternative approach on foot is to follow the track between two white posts at the entrance to San Carlos farm, 1km out of Es Mercadal on the Camí d'en Kane (➤ 19).

The simple courtyard is peaceful and attractive – an old well, an olive tree, a 16th-century stone tower, a low whitewashed refectory. You enter the church through a pretty porch with several arches and dozens of potted plants. Even when you get inside the 17th-century Renaissance church, there is little adornment – a plain white dome, tapestries on the walls, a 1943 altarpiece with a statue of the Virgin with the legendary bull at her feet. This is La Verge del Toro, the chief focus of pilgrimage. Mass is said here at 11AM each Sunday and the bishop holds a service each May to bless the fields on the island.

From the terrace and car park there are sea views on all four sides. Look down from the terrace over neat vegetable and herb gardens which are tended by the community of nuns who still live on Monte Toro.

Top **25**

22

Naveta des Tudons

The oldest roofed building in Spain – a Bronze Age burial chamber restored to its former glory in the 20th century.

Of all the prehistoric monuments on Menorca, this is probably the most visited. Until the 1950s it was dishevelled and overgrown; for centuries it had been used as a cattle-shed, but it was fully restored in 1959–60 and again in 1975.

The word *naveta* describes a burial chamber, built in the shape of an upturned boat. Most are horseshoe-shaped in design, with a low, narrow entrance at the straight end and a small antechamber leading into the main burial chamber. Some, like this, were built on two storeys; the bodies were left to decompose upstairs and the bones were subsequently transferred to the ground floor ossuary. Excavations in the 1950s revealed at least 100 corpses in Naveta des Tudons, some with bronze bracelets still around their arm-bones.

Navetas are unique to Menorca – of around 45 remaining, this is in the best condition. It is 14m long, 6m wide and around 4m high. Although a notice warns you not to disturb the stones by climbing, you can enter the *naveta* on hands and knees for a close look at the main chamber, supported by stone columns. You may even think you can smell the bones.

Because it is on the main road so close to Ciutadella, Naveta des Tudons attracts a large number of visitors. Come here early in the morning or late in the afternoon to catch some of the atmosphere and history of this place.

INFORMATION

- B2
- On Maó–Ciutadella road, 4km from Ciutadella
- Free access
- None

One of Menorca's Bronze Age burial chambers

Top **25**

23

S'Albufera des Grau

INFORMATION

- E2
- Free access to national park
- At Es Grau (€–€€)
- Buses from Maó to Es Grau in summer
- Boat trips to Illa d'en Colom and cruises around S'Albufera Park in summer ☎ 971 35 98 67
- S'Albufera Park reception centre offers guided walks 11AM Sat
  ☎ 971 35 24 44

A protected wetland area close to the east coast that acts as an important refuge for aquatic birds.

There used to be many more areas of wetland around the Menorcan coast, but most were drained for agriculture by the British or reclaimed for tourist *urbanizacións* in the 1960s. Of those that survive, S'Albufera is the largest and most important. A 70-hectare lagoon is separated from the sea by a barrier of sand, creating an area of salt-water marshes beside a freshwater lake.

The shores of the lake make a peaceful place to stroll, with birdwatching hides and a boardwalk trail. In winter there are migrant colonies of osprey and booted eagles; in spring and autumn the lake attracts waders and wildfowl. Species regularly seen here include cormorants, herons, spoonbills and terns. You may also spot turtles, toads and snakes.

The lake is separated from the beach at Es Grau by pine woods and dunes. Es Grau is an old-fashioned seaside village, with fishing boats in the harbour and white houses down to the water's edge. The large beach is a perfect place to go with children, as the water is shallow all the way out to Illa d'en Colom, seen across a channel 400m out to sea.

In summer you can take boat trips to the island, where there is a choice between sunny or shady beaches. This is the largest of Menorca's offshore islands; there is evidence of early habitation, with Roman ruins and a Byzantine church. The island, home to a protected species of lizard, is now part of the S'Albufera Park, the focus of Menorca's Biosphere Reserve.

S'Albufera is at the centre of the UNESCO Biosphere Reserve on Menorca

Top **25**

24

Son Bou

A long stretch of fine sandy beach with marshes, caves and an early Christian church.

Much of the south coast is made up of small, indented coves; Son Bou could hardly be more different. The longest beach on Menorca, it has almost 3km of pale golden sand, a sunbather's dream with facilities from beach bars to water-skiing and windsurfing. The water shelves gently and swimming is generally safe, but there are occasional dangerous currents so you should look out for the red and green flags. The beach is so long that it rarely gets crowded; it is always possible, especially at the western end, to find your own secluded spot.

At the east end of the beach, beneath two ugly hotels, is one of Menorca's more remarkable ancient monuments – a 5th-century Christian basilica, discovered in 1953. Similar to North African churches of the same period, it has three naves divided by pillars and a huge font, carved from a single stone. When you realise how long it lay hidden beneath the sand, it makes you wonder what further treasures are still waiting to be uncovered.

In the cliffs above the basilica are some large prehistoric burial caves, used as summer houses by Menorcan families. Climb up to these caves for the best views over the beach. Above the west end of the beach, separated by marshland, is the purpose-built resort of Sant Jaume Mediterrani. This has everything you could want for a family holiday – pools, shops, discos, plus the popular Club San Jaime with its water-chutes and labyrinthine maze.

INFORMATION

- D3
- Bars and restaurants (€–€€)
- Buses from Maó to Son Bou and Club San Jaime in summer, plus a shuttle 'train' connecting the hotels to the beach
- Torre d'en Galmés (➤ 48)

Son Bou – a perfect beach for families

Top **25**

25

Torre d'en Galmés

An atmospheric abandoned village with Bronze Age monuments and views over the south coast.

INFORMATION

- D3
- Tue–Sat 10–8, Sun, Mon 10–2.30 in summer, free access in winter
- None
- Inexpensive
- Son Bou (➤ 47)

A glimpse of an ancient culture – the remains of the prehistoric village of Torre d'en Galmés

The extensive prehistoric settlement of Torre d'en Galmés contains several well-preserved Talaiotic buildings. Most of it dates from around 1400 BC, though there is an even older sepulchre near by and evidence of habitation until Roman and perhaps medieval times.

Get there by following the signs from the Alaior–Son Bou road. As soon as you leave this road, the three *talaiots* are visible in the distance, 2km away down a country lane. A paved road leads around the site, making this the one prehistoric site in Menorca which is accessible to wheelchairs and pushchairs, though the path is bumpy in places and there is no access to the *taula* precinct.

Besides the three *talaiots*, there is a *taula* whose horizontal stone has collapsed, enabling you to appreciate its design, with a carefully hollowed-out centre to fit on top of the vertical stone. (It is possible that the hollow was enlarged at a later date for use as a Roman sarcophagus.) Near by is the best-preserved example of a hypostyle chamber, a roofed building with columns, possibly used as a dwelling but more likely as a sheep shelter or grain store. There is also an ingenious water storage and filtration system, probably Roman, with channels dug into the rock beneath a large flat surface.

This is a peaceful spot, with wild flowers growing among the ruins and views stretching from Monte Toro (➤ 44) to the south coast.

MENORCA's
best

Remote Beaches *50*

Viewpoints & Scenic Spots *51*

Historic Buildings *52*

Town & City Sights *53*

Beach Resorts *54*

Archaeological Sites *55*

Children's Attractions *56–57*

Unusual Outdoor Attractions *58*

Free Attractions *59*

Places to Have Lunch by the Sea *60*

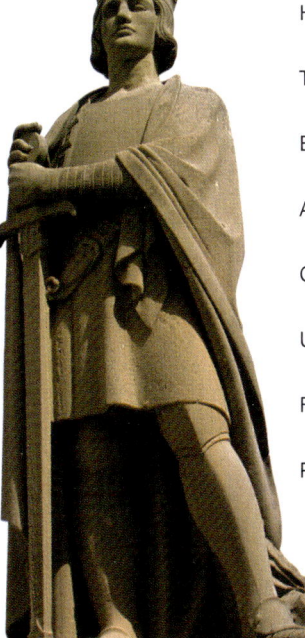

Menorca's Best

Remote Beaches

In the Top 25
- **4** CALA D'ALGAIARENS (➤ 27)
- **5** CALA EN TURQUETA (➤ 28)
- **6** CALA MACARELLA (➤ 29)
- **9** CALA PREGONDA (➤ 31)
- **10** CALES COVES (➤ 33)

ARENAL DE SON SAURA
This is one of Menorca's prettiest beaches and one of the hardest to reach. To get there by car you have to cross farmland and in summer the farmer levies a toll. Alternatively, walk from Cala En Turqueta (1 hour) on the coastal footpath from Son Xoriguer to Cala Santa Galdana. It is worth the effort – you will find two stretches of white sand, hidden behind fragrant pine woods. There are no facilities so take a picnic.
B3 None — Trips from Ciutadella and Cala En Bosc in summer

CALA DEL PILAR
This is a wild, lonely, beautiful spot that nevertheless gets busy at weekends. Reach it by leaving the main Maó to Ciutadella road from the 34km point beneath the Castillo Menorca factory shop; when the tarmac road runs out, pass through some gates on to farmland and park in a grove of oak and pine. Walk through the woods for 40 minutes and you emerge on to reddish dunes; from here, you scramble down to the beach.
C2 None

A sandy path leads through the woods to Cala del Pilar

CALA ESCORXADA
The owner of the land behind this cove has denied access to ramblers, so the beach has become even more remote than it was. Get there by boat, or by a long (two hours minimum) and difficult walk from Cala Santa Galdana (➤ 32). Cala Escorxada is typical of the south coast – limestone cliffs, pine woods and a beach of soft white sand; it is good for snorkelling.
C3 None

CALA MITJANA
Best reached on foot from Cala Santa Galdana (➤ 32). The walk takes about 30 minutes, passing the rocky cove of Cala Mitjaneta before arriving at a deep sandy beach surrounded by cliffs full of caves.
C3 None — To Cala Santa Galdana (summer), then walk

CALA TREBALÚGER
A popular mooring for yachts and pleasure boats in summer, the cove can only be reached on foot by a walk of about 1½ hours from Cala Santa Galdana (➤ 32), followed by a scramble down to the beach.
C3 None — Boat trips from Cala En Bosc and Cala Santa Galdana (summer)

Menorca's Best

Viewpoints & Scenic Spots

In the Top 25
- **6** CALA MACARELLA (➤ 29)
- **9** CALA SANTA GALDANA (➤ 32)
- **10** CALES COVES (➤ 33)
- **21** MONTE TORO (➤ 44)
- **25** TORRE D'EN GAUMÉS (➤ 48)

CALA D'ALCAUFAR
This small creek is classically Menorcan – fishermen's cottages reach down to the water's edge and the narrow, sheltered inlet is lined with boats and backed by a sandy beach. From the cliffs, a short walk leads to a headland crowned by a Martello tower.

🟥 F3 🍴 Bar/restaurant beside beach (€) 🚌 From Maó in summer

CALA DE SANT ESTEVE
St Stephen's Creek is named after the Christian martyr whose remains were said to have been buried here. On one side are the ruins of Fort Sant Felip (➤ 52); on the other the seven-sided Fort Marlborough, built by the British in the late 18th century. Fort Marlborough is now a museum – the special effects include explosions in the underground tunnels. Climb to the rooftop for more peaceful views.

🟥 F3 🍴 None ☎ Fort Malborough: 971 36 04 62 🕐 Tue–Sat 10–1, 5–8, Sun 10–1 💰 Moderate (free Sun)

CAP DE CAVALLERÍA
This headland at Menorca's northernmost point is one of the island's wild places. To get there you have to follow a potholed road across several kilometres of rocky moors. On the way you pass the tiny harbour of Sanitja, Menorca's third city in Roman times. Crossing cattle grids and passing through farm gates, eventually you reach the lighthouse at the end of the cape.

🟥 D1 🍴 Café

CAP DE FAVÀRITX
Stand on Menorca's northeastern tip when the *tramuntana* is blowing and you will appreciate the island's savage beauty. Waves crash against crumbling slate cliffs, below the solitary lighthouse.

🟥 F2 🍴 None 🔁 Cala Presili

SANTA AGUEDA
Menorca's third-highest hill once supported the island's most significant Roman fortress and the path to the summit takes you along the best-preserved Roman road in Menorca. To get there, take the Binisues road, signposted off the C721 3km west of Ferreries; after another 3km, park by an old white schoolhouse and go through the gate.

🟥 C2 🍴 None 🔁 Binisues

The absence of a beach means that Cala de Sant Esteve has remained peaceful and uncrowded

Menorca's Best

Historic Buildings

In the Top 25

■ **CHURCHES AND HOUSES IN ALAIOR** (➤ 24)
■ **CIUTADELLA'S MUSEU MUNICIPAL** (➤ 35)
■ **MAÓ'S ESGLÉSIA DEL CARME** (➤ 41)

CIUTADELLA'S CATEDRAL
Ciutadella has been Menorca's religious capital since Arab times; when Alfonso III conquered the island in 1287, one of his first acts was to have the main mosque reconsecrated as a church. The Catalan-Gothic structure took shape over the next 75 years, though part of the old mosque still remains in the ramp of the north tower, reminiscent of an Islamic minaret. The church finally gained its cathedral status in 1795, when a bishopric was restored to Ciutadella. The cathedral is currently closed for repairs until late 2005.
🛈 A2 ✉ Plaça de la Catedral ☎ 971 38 07 39 🕐 Closed until late 2005 🍴 Near by (€–€€) 💶 Free ↔ Plaça des Born (➤ 36)

CIUTADELLA'S PALAU SALORD
The streets of the old city are filled with 17th-century palaces such as this one, built by Menorca's aristocratic families when they moved to Ciutadella from their country estates. Most are still owned by the original families. Among the riches on display here are antique furniture, tapestries and oil paintings, gilded mirrors and a frescoed ballroom.
🛈 A2 ✉ Carrer Major del Born 9 🕐 Apr–Oct: Mon–Sat 10–2 🍴 In Plaça des Born (€–€€) 💶 Cheap

FORT MARLBOROUGH
(See Cala de Sant Esteve, ➤ 51)

FORT SANT FELIP
Not much remains of this once impregnable fortress, begun at the southern entrance to Maó harbour following the Turkish raids in the 16th century. The British strengthened it in the 18th century, using the most modern military engineering techniques to create a network of tunnels which allowed a whole garrison of soldiers to live underground.
🛈 F3 🍴 None ☎ For details of guided tours: 971 36 21 00

MAÓ'S SANTA MARIA CHURCH
Maó main church was begun soon after the Catalan conquest, then rebuilt in neo-classical style in the 18th century in a gesture of defiance to the island's British Protestant rulers. Most people come here to see (or hear) the organ, built by the Swiss maker Johann Kyburz and imported from Barcelona during the Napoleonic Wars with the help of the British.
🛈 E3 ✉ Plaça Constitució, Maó ☎ 971 36 39 49 🍴 In Plaça Bastió

Palau Salord is typical of the noble mansions that dominate the old town of Ciutadella

FORTALESA DE LA MOLA
The fortress at La Mola, guarding the entrance to Maó harbour, was built in 1848 following the destruction of Fort Sant Felip (➤ opposite). During the Civil War and the Franco dictatorship, it became known as an infamous military and political prison. The army abandoned it in 1998 and it is now open for tours (allow 2 hours) to see the galleries, walls, casemates and gunpowder stores, as well as two 38cm Vickers cannon.
🛈 F3 ☎ 971 362100
🕐 Nov–May: Sun 11AM; Jun and Oct, Tue 5PM and Sun 10AM; Jul–Sep, Tue, Wed, Fri 6PM, Sun 10AM 💶 Moderate

Menorca's Best

Town & City Sights

In the Top 25
- 🎯 **CIUTADELLA'S PLAÇA DES BORN (► 36)**
- 🎯 **MAÓ'S PLAÇA DE S'ESPLANADA (► 43)**

CIUTADELLA'S PASSEIG MARÍTIM
This wide promenade, completed in 1997, follows the seafront around the peninsula from the small beach at Cala des Degollador to the marina. This is the place to come at dusk to watch the sun set over the sea and join the locals on their evening *passeig*.
🗺 A2 🍽 At the harbour (€€–€€€) 🏛 Castell Sant Nicolau

CIUTADELLA'S SES VOLTES
This pedestrian alley, with its Moorish arches, is also named after the local historian José-Maria Quadrado, and is the focal point of Ciutadella's social life.
🗺 A2 🍽 Restaurants and bars (€–€€)

ES CASTELL
Founded by the British during their second occupation, and originally named Georgetown after George III, Es Castell retains the feel of a British colonial town. The main square, Plaça de S'Esplanada, is the former British parade ground and is now home to a military museum. Near by is the attractive harbour of Cales Fonts.
🗺 F3 🍽 Wide choice in Cales Fonts (€–€€) 🚌 Buses from Maó

ES MERCADAL
The name hints at the town's origins in the 14th century as a market halfway between Maó and Ciutadella. Much later it was the setting for a defining moment in Menorcan history, when in 1706 the supporters of the Austrian archduke Charles, pretender to the Spanish throne, declared him king – providing the pretext for the subsequent British invasion. Nowadays Es Mercadal is a quiet town of plain white houses in the shadow of Menorca's highest mountain (► 44), manufacturing *abarcas*, (sandals with soles made from recycled tyres) and the almond biscuits known as *amargas* and *carquinyols*.
🗺 D2 🚌 From Maó and Ciutadella 🎉 *Festa de Sant Martí*, third Sun in Jul. Craft market Thu evenings in summer

SANT LLUÍS
Founded by the French in 1761 to provide housing for their troops, the town is laid out in a grid style around a series of attractive squares; it was named after Louis IX, to whom the huge, whitewashed, buttressed church is dedicated. A blue and white windmill, Molí de Dalt, seen as you enter the town from Maó, has been turned into a small folk museum.
🗺 E3 🚌 From Maó 🎉 *Festa de Sant Lluís*, last weekend in Aug

Carrer Major in Es Mercadal – the house with the flags flying is the town hall

Menorca's Best

Beach Resorts

THE STORY OF XOROI'S CAVE

Xoroi was a legendary Berber pirate who was shipwrecked at Cala En Porter. He abducted a local girl and kept her in his cave for 10 years, during which time she produced four children. When his footprints in the snow gave him away the girl was rescued by her family, and Xoroi threw himself into the sea.

Chic and cheerful – Cala En Bosc

In the Top 25

CALA SANTA GALDANA (➤ 32)
SON BOU (➤ 47)

ARENAL D'EN CASTELL
The most westerly and brashest of the trio of resorts north of Alaior (the name means 'sandy place'). The near-circular bay with its arc of fine sand backing on to dunes and pine-fringed cliffs is rather spoilt by the two enormous modern hotels towering over the beach. Windsurfing, water-skiing, pedal boat and motorboat hire are all available.
 E2 Bars and restaurants From Maó and Fornells in summer

CALA EN BOSC
Life in fashionable Cala En Bosc revolves around the marina, built on the site of a drained wetland. Small boats can enter the marina through a narrow channel; this is also a departure point for cruises to the remoter coves along the south coast. Nearby Son Xoriguer, with its large twin beaches, is a centre for watersports.
 A3 Choice of restaurants From Ciutadella in summer

CALA EN PORTER
A wide beach leads to a narrow cove where turquoise water shimmers between tall limestone cliffs. A *barranc*, or ravine, enters the sea via the marshland at the back of the beach. The most unusual bar is Cova d'en Xoroi, set in a natural cave.
 D3 Bars and restaurants From Maó in summer

CALA MESQUIDA
The old watchtower here was the site of the Duc de Crillon's landing with a Franco-Spanish invasion force in 1781. There is very little modern development and the village feels more Menorcan than touristy.
 F3 Es Cap Roig

SANT TOMÀS
Virtually a continuation of the beach at Son Bou (➤ 47), separated from it by a pair of low headlands. In 1989 a freak storm blew away all the sand from the beach; what you see now has been imported.
 C3 Restaurants and bars Buses from Maó, Ciutadella and Es Migjorn Gran in summer

SON PARC
An *urbanización*, with a golf course and hundreds of identical apartments, leads to this perfect beach. The water is shallow, there are pedaloes for hire, and the dunes and pinewoods offer relief from the sun.
 D2 Bars and restaurants, including beach bar in summer
 Buses from Maó and Fornells in summer

Menorca's Best

Archaeological Sites

In the Top 25

7 CALA MORELL (➤ 30)
10 CALES COVES (➤ 33)
22 NAVETA DES TUDONS (➤ 45)
24 SON BOU (➤ 47)
25 TORRE D'EN GALMÉS (➤ 48)

SA TORRETA (➤ 58)

SANT AGUSTÍ VELL (➤ 58)

SON CATLAR
Menorca's largest megalithic settlement, on the road from Ciutadella to Arenal, was built around 1800 BC and occupied right up to the Middle Ages. The surrounding wall of massive stones is some 900m in circumference. A doorway on the north side of the wall leads to a *taula* precinct.
🅱 B2 🕓 Apr–Oct daily 9.30–sunset, free access in winter
🕓 Moderate ❓ Multi-lingual information boards on site

TALATÍ DE DALT
Talatí de Dalt blends so well into its surroundings that it is hard to tell which of the piles of stones are ancient and which modern. An olive tree grows inside the *taula* precinct; bushes sprout out of a *talaiot* and standing stones are scattered around a field.
🅴 E3 ✉ Signposted off Maó–Ciutadella road, 4km from Maó
🕓 Apr–Oct daily 10–8, free access in winter 🕓 Moderate 🍴 None

TORELLÓ
Two sites separated by 300m and a millennium of history are found in the shadow of a modern airport. The *talaiot* is visible from incoming planes. The 6th-century basilica, Es Fornàs de Torelló, was discovered in 1956 by a farmer ploughing his fields. Parts of the altar survive, as does the baptismal font.
🅴 E3 ✉ Off the Maó–Sant Climent road 🕓 Free access 🍴 None

TORRALBA D'EN SALORD
The remains of a complete village lie here, including a *taula*, a *talaiot* and a well, 46m deep with nine flights of steps and a stone handrail hewn out of the rock.
🅳 D3 ✉ On Alaior–Cala En Porter road 🕓 Jun–Sep daily 10–8; Oct–May Mon–Sat 10–1, 3–6 🍴 Kiosk 🕓 Moderate

TREPUCÓ
The *taula* here, 4m high, is the tallest in Menorca. The complex is surrounded by a star-shaped wall, built by the Duc de Crillon in 1782 when the French were laying siege to Fort Sant Felip (➤ 52) and used Trepucó as their base.
🅴 E3 ✉ Signposted off Maó–Sant Lluis road 🕓 Free access 🍴 None

Was it built by giants? The outer wall of Son Catlar

PIECE IT ALL TOGETHER

After exploring Menorca's archaeological sites, visit the Museu de Menorca to fill in the missing links in your knowledge of the island's history.
Coins, pottery and funerary objects from several different cultures are gathered under one roof, together with the island's largest collection of fine arts. Among the objects on display is a complete skeleton of *Myotragus balearicus*, a goat-like mammal that once lived on Menorca but became extinct with the arrival of man.
✉ Plaça des Monestir, Maó
🕓 Apr–Oct Tue–Sat 10–2, 6–8.30, Sun 10–2; Nov–Mar Tue–Sat 9.30–2, Sun 10–2
🕓 Inexpensive (free Sun)

Menorca's Best

Children's Attractions

LOOKING AFTER CHILDREN

Small children are particularly vulnerable to the sun and need to be protected; apply a high-factor sun block regularly, especially after swimming. If you need a child seat in your hire car, make sure to book it in advance and check it carefully on arrival. The same goes for cots and high chairs in hotels and apartments. Finally, don't forget to check that your balcony railings are secure.

A lifeguard keeps watch over the holidaymakers at Club San Jaime

Menorca is a very child-friendly society. Like other Mediterranean people, the Spanish are known for their love of children and no one is going to complain if you take your child out to a good restaurant.

Many hotels have children's nurseries and baby-sitting services and package-tour operators often lay on children's activities. Every resort has a playground, and often these are found in hotels too. Some hotels have mini-golf circuits and children's pools.

Most children are happy just being on the beach. Menorca has plenty of child-friendly beaches, with safe, shallow water, Red Cross posts and red warning flags which are flown when the sea is dangerous.

Children will enjoy the 'road trains' which make a circuit of certain resorts in summer. Other activities which particularly appeal to children include:

ADVENTURE PARKS AND PLAYGROUNDS

AQUAPARK
This waterpark near Ciutadella has waterslides, trampolines, bouncy castles, playgrounds, pools, video games, go-karts and a pizzeria.
✚ A2 ✉ Avinguda de los Delfines, Cala En Blanes ☎ 971 38 82 51
🕐 May–Oct: daily 10:30–6

AQUAROCK
Thrills and spills including the Kamikaze waterslide plus swimming pools and wave machines at this waterpark south of Ciutadella.
✚ A3 ✉ Cala En Bosc ☎ 971 387822 🕐 May–Oct: daily 10.30–6

CLUB ESCOLA MENORQUINA
The equestrian show here has carriage rides, dressage displays and performances of prancing and rearing. Children are offered donkey rides during the interval.
✚ C2 ✉ Carretera Ferreries–Cala Santa Galdana, km0.5, Ferreries
☎ 971 37 34 97 🕐 May–Oct: Wed, Sun 8:30PM

CLUB SAN JAIME
A wealth of activities to keep little ones amused, including a swimming pool, a water-chute and a remarkable interlocking wooden maze which can be rearranged to get harder as you go along. The complex is arranged around attractively landscaped gardens with views over the marshes and out to sea.
✚ D3 ✉ Sunt Jaume Mediterrani, Son Bou ☎ 971 37 27 87
🕐 May–Oct: daily 10–7

HORT DE LLUCAITX PARK
Countryside recreation centre with activities for kids

Menorca's Best

of all ages – pony-trekking, bike hire, cart rides, playgrounds, trampolines, plus farm animals to feed.
✚ D2 ✉ Carretera Maó–Fornells, km17, Son Parc ☎ 607 900 999
🕐 May–Oct: daily 10–8. Sat and Sun only in winter

PARC D'ES FREGINAL
A delightful urban playground, with orchards, gardens, fountains, ponds and swings, right in the centre of town. There is also a children's playground on nearby Plaça de S'Esplanada.
✚ ✉ Entrance on Costa d'en Deià, Maó 🕐 Daily 8–8

BEACHES
The following beaches are particularly suitable for children: Arenal d'en Castell, Binibèquer, Cala Blanca, Cala d'Alcaufar, Cala En Porter, Cala Santa Galdana, Cala Santandría, Es Grau, Son Bou, Son Parc. All these beaches have shallow water, plenty of sand, and are easily reached by car. You can rent pedal boats in summer; some of the larger beaches (such as Cala Santa Galdana and Son Parc) also have canoes and motor boats for hire.

BOAT TRIPS
Children often enjoy the thrill of the open water and there are numerous boat excursions around the Menorcan coast in summer. Services vary throughout the season so it is best to ask or to look for notices on the quayside. A popular option is a full-day trip to a cove that cannot be reached by road; the price often includes lunch, usually a *paella* cooked on the beach. Another option is to charter your own yacht or motor boat and simply set off to explore.
Popular boat trips include: Cala En Bosc to Arenal de Son Saura and Cala En Turqueta; Cala Santa Galdana to Cala Trebalúger; and Ciutadella to Arenal de Son Saura and Cala En Turqueta.

RESTAURANTS

LOS TOBOGANES
The giant waterslide and the crazy-golf course are ideal for keeping children entertained while you enjoy Italian food overlooking the beach.
✉ Cala Blanca ☎ 971 38 51 68

TOBOGÁN
Pizzeria plus mini-golf, a pool, a playground and a waterslide.
✉ Passeig del Riu, Cala Santa Galdana
☎ 971 15 46 16

FAMILY OUTINGS

As well as the attractions listed here, children will enjoy the trotting races at Maó and Ciutadella (➤ 81), the Molí de Dalt windmill at Sant Lluís (➤ 53) and the boat tours of Maó harbour (➤ 42).

Timeless pleasures on the beach at Punta Prima

Menorca's Best

Unusual Outdoor Attractions

A sandstone cathedral – the quarry at S'Hostal, near Ciutadella

S'HOSTAL
Menorca's most unusual tourist attraction is a disused sandstone quarry outside Ciutadella which has been turned into a monument to the island's history and traditions of quarrying. Traditionally sandstone was extracted by hammer and chisel; the few remaining quarries use circular saws which dig deep into the ground, creating vertical walls of white stone. The quarry closed in 1994; it was bought up by Líthica and reopened the following year. You can walk around a 'labyrinth of orchards' in the old quarry, now being turned into a garden, then descend to the giant white amphitheatre of the modern quarry, 30m deep, where on weekdays workmen give displays of quarrying. Líthica has ambitious plans for this site – a sculpture park, a museum and visitor centre, a concert auditorium beneath the sheer white walls. An industrial wasteland has been creatively transformed into an unexpectedly special place.

🚩 B2 ✉ 2km from Ciutadella on Camí Vell de Maó ☎ 971 48 15 78
🕐 Summer: daily 9:30–sunset. Winter: free access 🍴 None
💰 Moderate

SA TORRETA
One of the few Talaiotic sites in northern Menorca is also one of the hardest to reach; the best way is the walk from Es Grau (➤ 18). Overgrown and evocative, a complete *taula* 4m high is surrounded by standing stones on the edge of a farm. Tests show that this was built 1,000 years after the *taulas* at Son Catlar and Trepucó (➤ 55), proving that the Talaiotic culture was certainly not short-lived.

🚩 E2 🕐 Free access 🍴 None ↔ S'Albufera des Grau (➤ 46)

SANT AGUSTÍ VELL
This is one of the hardest of Menorca's prehistoric sites to find but that makes the effort all the more rewarding, and you will probably be alone with your thoughts when you get there. Take the road from Es Migjorn Gran to Sant Tomàs; after 1km, an unsigned track to your right leads to the farm of Sant Agustí. Park just off the main road and walk along this track. At the farm gates, go right, through a gate marked *cuevas*; when you see a pair of litter bins you know that you have reached the site. The main attraction here is a large *talaiot* with a beamed roof of olive and juniper wood; once they would all have been like this but this is the only one which survives. The village was strategically situated at the head of the Binigaus gorge; it can also be reached by climbing from the Cova des Coloms (➤ 37).

🚩 C3 🕐 Free access 🍴 None 🚌 To Es Migjorn Gran from Maó and Ferreries

Menorca's Best

Free Attractions

AJUNTAMENT DE MAÓ
You can wander inside Maó's town hall to see portraits of former governors, along with a sculpted image of Saint Sebastian, patron saint of Maó. The clock on the façade was a gift from the first British governor, Sir Richard Kane.
✚ E3 ✉ Plaça de Constitució, Maó ☎ 971 36 98 00 ⏰ Office hours

ATENEU DE MAÓ
Maó has a rich intellectual tradition, perhaps a result of the exposure to so many foreign cultures and ideas. The focus of the city's intellectual life is this scientific, literary and artistic association, founded in 1905. The museum, kept open by devoted scholars, contains maps, ceramics, watercolours and fossils.
✚ E3 ✉ Sa Rovellada de Dalt 25, Maó ☎ 971 36 05 53
⏰ Mon–Sat 10–2, 4–10

CASTELL SANT NICOLAU
This 17th-century defence tower on the waterfront in Ciutadella is used for displays on environmental themes and occasional art exhibitions. Each evening people come to watch the sun set over the sea, with the mountains of Mallorca in the distance.
✚ A2 ✉ Passeig Marítim, Ciutadella ⏰ Tue–Sat 10–1:30, 5–8

MUSEU DEL PINTOR TORRENT
The works of José Torrent (1904–90), a painter known as 'the Van Gogh of Menorca', are on display in this intimate museum in his home town of Ciutadella.
✚ A2 ✉ Carrer San Rafel 11, Ciutadella ⏰ Mon–Fri 11–1, 7:30–9:30, Sat, Sun 8AM–9:30PM

XORIGUER
Menorca's leading gin distillery is open for tastings, with no obligation to buy. As well as the gin, you can try various gin-based herbal liqueurs with ingredients ranging from camomile to carob.
✚ E3 ✉ Moll de Ponent 93, Maó ☎ 971 36 21 97 ⏰ May–Oct: Mon–Fri 8–7, Sat 9–1; Nov–Apr: Mon–Fri 9–1, 4–7

ARCHAEOLOGICAL SITES
Few of Menorca's prehistoric sites have been developed for tourism, and the majority stand undisturbed in the middle of farmland. Access is free, but as you are on private land, remember to respect the property of the farmer by leaving everything exactly as you found it. For details of archaeological sites ➤ 55 and 58.

The gin distillery at Xoriguer

Menorca's Best

Places to Have Lunch by the Sea

In the Top 25
- **CALA MACARELLA (▶ 29)**
- **CALA MORELL (▶ 30)**
- **MAÓ HARBOUR (▶ 42)**
- **SON BOU (▶ 47)**

BINIMEL-LÀ (€€)
Fabulous setting high above the dunes and beach.
✚ C2 ✉ Platja de Binimel-là ☎ 971 359275

CAFÉ BALEAR (€€)
Fresh seafood beside the harbour where the fishermen unload their catch.
✚ A2 ✉ Passeig de Sant Joan 17, Ciutadella ☎ 971 380005

CA'N DELIO (€€)
A good place to enjoy grilled fish beside the sea.
✚ F3 ✉ Cales Fonts 38, Es Castell ☎ 971 35 17 11

EL MIRADOR (€€)
The perfect setting on a terrace overlooking the sea.
✉ Over the footbridge from Hotel Audax, Cala Santa Galdana ☎ 971 15 45 03

ES CAP ROIG (€€)
Simply cooked fresh fish, in a spectacular setting looking out to sea. Popular with locals.
✚ F3 ✉ Cala Mesquida (just before the village on the road from Maó) ☎ 971 18 83 83

ES PLA (€€€)
Where the king comes to eat *caldereta de langosta*.
✚ D2 ✉ Passeig des Pla, Fornells ☎ 971 37 66 55

LOS BUCANEROS (€€)
Old-style *chiringuito* (beach bar) with a shaded terrace.
✚ E4 ✉ Platja de Binibèquer ⏰ May–Oct 10–8

Enjoying a meal at one of Cala Blanca's waterside restaurants

SUSY (€€)
Come here for generous portions of Spanish cuisine, in a restaurant by the beach. Dishes include grilled squid, grilled sole or roast chicken with chips.
✚ B3 ✉ Cala Macarella ☎ 971 35 94 67 ⏰ Summer: daily 10:30–6

MENORCA
where to…

EAT
In Maó *62–63*
In Ciutadella *64–65*
Around the Island *66–69*

STAY
In Maó & Ciutadella *70*
Around the Island *71–73*

SHOP
Food & Drink *74*
Arts, Books & Gifts *75*
Leather & Jewellery *76–77*

BE ENTERTAINED
Art Galleries, Cinemas & Theatres *78*
Music & Nightlife *79*
Discos *80*
Spectator & Participatory Sport *81*
Watersports *82–83*

Where to Eat

In Maó

PRICES

Prices are approximate, based on a three-course meal for one, without drinks and service:
€ = under €15
€€ = €15–€30
€€€ = over €30
Most restaurants serve a *menú del día* (➤ 65) at lunchtime (and sometimes in the evening) which will usually work out much cheaper. It is normal practice to add about 10 per cent to the bill as a tip.

AMADEUS (€)
Coffee, sandwiches, snacks and drinks – a great place for people-watching in a corner of the main square.
✉ Plaça de S'Esplanada 57 ☎ 971 350792 🕒 Daily 8AM–11PM

AMATXO (€€)
Trendy Basque bar just off Plaça de S'Esplanada offering a choice of *pintxos* (open sandwiches) or complete meals. Also on the waterfront at Moll de Llevant 115.
✉ Sa Rovellada de Dalt 20 ☎ 971 353848 🕒 Mon–Sat 12–12

AMERICAN BAR (€)
Busy meeting place in the heart of the pedestrian shopping district.
✉ Plaça Reial 8 ☎ 971 36 18 22 🕒 7AM until late

ANDAIRA (€€€)
Creative Mediterranean cuisine in a town house with a lemon-shaded courtyard.
✉ Carrer des Forn 61 ☎ 971 36 68 17 🕒 Dinner only, Mar–Sep

CASANOVA (€€)
Fresh pasta and wood-fired pizzas at a buzzing waterfront trattoria.
✉ Moll de Ponent 15 ☎ 971 354169 🕒 Lunch and dinner, Tue–Sun

CASA SEXTO (€€)
Fishy *tapas* and seafood specialities – the owner flies in fresh seafood from his native Galicia and cooks it in sea water.
✉ Carrer Vassallo 2 ☎ 971 36 84 07 🕒 Lunch, dinner. Closed Sun and Mon lunch

EL GUALLACÁN (€€)
Romantic Argentinian restaurant on the promenade offering a choice of *tapas* or grilled meats.
✉ Moll de Llevant 139 ☎ 971 360528 🕒 Lunch and dinner, Tue–Sun

EL VIEJO ALMACEN (€€)
Trendy waterfront *tapas* bar specialising in barbecued meat and vegetables. Try the *pintxos*, nibbles of bread topped with ham, anchovies or cheese.
✉ Moll de Llevant 75 ☎ 971 36 89 52 🕒 Tue–Sun 12–12

ES FOSQUET (€€€)
Intimate harbourside fish restaurant in a cave with whitewashed walls and an outdoor terrace. Daily selection of fresh fish.
✉ Moll de Llevant 256 ☎ 971 35 00 58 🕒 Dinner, May–Sep, Tue–Sun

GREGAL (€€)
Locals consider this one of the best harbourside restaurants in Cala Figuera.
✉ Moll de Llevant 306 ☎ 971 36 66 06 🕒 Lunch, dinner

IL PORTO (€€)
Pizzas, barbecues and grilled vegetables on the waterfront.
✉ Moll de Llevant 225 ☎ 971 35 44 26 🕒 Lunch, dinner (dinner only Jul, Aug)

ITAKE (€€)
One of the few waterfront restaurants not to concentrate on fish. Fashionable and offbeat.
✉ Moll de Llevant 317 ☎ 971

Where to Eat

35 45 70 🕒 Lunch Tue–Sun, dinner Tue–Sat

JÀGARO (€€€)
Fresh seafood and views from the harbourside terrace are the attractions at this top-notch Cala Figuera restaurant.
✉ Moll de Llevant 334
☎ 971 36 23 90 🕒 Lunch, dinner daily. Closed Sun in winter

LA MINERVA (€€€)
Upmarket restaurant set in an old flour mill, with six different dining rooms and a floating terrace. Mediterranean nouvelle cuisine as well as traditional lobster *paella*.
✉ Moll de Ponent 87 ☎ 971 35 19 95 🕒 Lunch, dinner

L'ARPÓ (€€)
Pretty waterfront bistro specialising in simple fresh fish and *paella*.
✉ Moll de Llevant 124 ☎ 971 36 98 44 🕒 Lunch, dinner

LA SIRENA (€€–€€€)
Bistro serving *comida integral* (whole food cooking), with organic meat, fish and vegetarian dishes. Asian and Mediterranean influences.
✉ Moll de Llevant 199
☎ 971 35 07 40 🕒 Dinner. Closed Tue

LATITUD 40° (€€)
Late-night harbourside bar specialising in *tapas*, grilled vegetables and cheese.
✉ Moll de Llevant 265 ☎ 971 36 41 76 🕒 Mon–Sat 7PM–3AM

MARIVENT (€€€)
Probably the best of the many harbourside restaurants at Cala Figuera.
✉ Moll de Llevant 314 ☎ 971 36 98 01 🕒 Lunch, dinner. Closed Tue

MESON DEL PUERTO (€€)
Classic Basque cuisine in a lively area beside the ferry port.
✉ Moll de Ponent 66 ☎ 971 35 29 03 🕒 Closed Sun

MIRADOR CAFÉ (€)
Wonderful harbour views – just the place for a scenic sandwich or snack.
✉ Plaça d'Espanya 2 ☎ 971 352107 🕒 Mon–Sat 10AM–2AM

NASHVILLE (€€)
The ultimate in cultural confusion – pizzas, German and Tex-Mex dishes in this 'beer and soundhouse' by the sea.
✉ Moll de Llevant 145 ☎ 971 36 79 56 🕒 Lunch, dinner

ROMA (€)
Fashionable, reasonably priced pizzeria.
✉ Moll de Llevant 295 ☎ 971 35 37 77 🕒 Lunch, dinner. Closed Tue

S'ESPIGO (€€)
Small, stylish restaurant with a wide range of fish baked in sea salt.
✉ Moll de Llevant 267 ☎ 971 36 99 09 🕒 Closed Sun lunch

VARADERO (€€€)
Swish, expensive harbourside restaurant offering designer *paellas* and fish dishes such as monkfish casserole and oven-baked fish in a salt crust. Beside the jetty where cruise ships disembark.
✉ Moll de Llevant 4 ☎ 971 35 20 74 🕒 Lunch, dinner

OPENING TIMES

The Spanish like to eat late – many restaurants do not even open until 1:30 at lunchtime and 8:30 in the evening, and fill up an hour or two later. Most restaurants either close down for the winter or severely reduce their opening times, so it is always a good idea to check in advance. *Tapas* bars tend to be open throughout the day.

Where to Eat

In Ciutadella

TAPAS

Tapas are a Spanish institution. Originally a free 'lid' (*tapa*) of ham across a drink, nowadays they consist of small portions of everything from octopus to olives. Locals tend to eat *tapas* before going home for dinner, but several portions can make a filling meal in itself. And you don't have to look at a menu – just point to what you want in the cabinet.

ANTICO PIACERE (€€)
Traditional Italian restaurant near the market offering classic dishes such as spaghetti carbonara, *osso bucco*, veal cooked in milk, and tiramisu for dessert.
✉ Carrer Sant Isidre 7 ☎ 971 482072 ⊙ Lunch, dinner, Mon–Sat

AURORA (€)
Fishy *tapas* and fresh seafood on a lively square where the old town meets the new.
✉ Plaça Alfons III 3 ☎ 971 38 00 29 ⊙ Lunch, dinner

CAFÉ BALEAR (€€)
The perfect setting for lunch by the harbour; plenty of fresh shellfish plus steaks and *carpaccio* of veal.
✉ Passeig de Sant Joan 17 ☎ 971 38 00 05 ⊙ Lunch, dinner. Closed Sun in summer, Mon in winter

CAN LLUÍS (€€)
In the back streets around the market, this offers a fresh take on Menorcan cookery, with salt cod specialities, plates of ham and cheese, and creative Mediterranean cuisine.
✉ Carrer Alaior 22 ☎ 971 380154 ⊙ Lunch, dinner, Mon–Sat

CA'N NITO (€€)
Tapas bar on the edge of the Born with lots of fish dishes and charcoal-grilled steaks.
✉ Plaça des Born 11 ☎ 971 48 07 68 ⊙ All day

CASA MANOLO (€€€)
Top-notch fresh seafood and lobster dishes beside the harbour walls.
✉ Port de Ciutadella ☎ 971 38 00 03 ⊙ Lunch, dinner

CAS FERRER (€€€)
An old blacksmith's forge has been converted into a tasteful terrace restaurant, offering a changing menu of modern Mediterranean dishes.
✉ Carrer Portal de Sa Font 16 ☎ 971 480784 ⊙ Lunch, dinner, Tue–Sat

CLUB NÁUTICO (€€)
Serious fish dishes in the yacht club overlooking the port.
✉ Camí Baix, beneath Passeig Marítim ☎ 971 38 27 73 ⊙ Lunch, dinner

DON GIACOMO (€€)
Italian-Mediterranean cuisine, including wood-fired pizzas and Catalan-inspired meat dishes, served in a town house with vaulted ceilings and stone walls.
✉ Carrer Nou de Juliol 5 ☎ 971 38 32 79 ⊙ Lunch, dinner

EL BRIBÓN (€€)
Down by the harbour it's a question of just taking your pick, but this seafood restaurant and *tapas* bar is better value than most.
✉ Port de Ciutadella ☎ 971 38 50 50 ⊙ Lunch, dinner

EL HORNO (€€)
Intimate French basement restaurant near the Plaça des Born.
✉ Carrer des Forn 12 ☎ 971 38 07 67 ⊙ Dinner, Apr–Oct

ES LLOC (€€€)
This hotel restaurant has an excellent reputation for

Where to Eat

creative Menorcan and Mediterranean cuisine. Seasonal menu.
✉ Hotel Sant Ignasi, Carretera de Cala Morell ☎ 971 38 55 75
🕐 Lunch, dinner in summer; weekends only in winter

LA GUITARRA (€€)

Classic Menorcan dishes, such as duck, roast lamb, snails, in an atmospheric cellar.
✉ Carrer Nostra Senyora dels Dolors 1 ☎ 971 38 13 55
🕐 Closed Sun

LA PAYESA (€€)

Large choice of seafood dishes including three different *paellas*. Plus a children's menu.
✉ Port de Ciutadella ☎ 971 38 00 21 🕐 Lunch, dinner

ORISTANO (€)

Fresh pasta and wood-fired pizzas in an old shoe factory overlooking the Pla de Sant Joan. Popular with a late-night crowd at weekends.
✉ Carrer Borja Moll 1 ☎ 971 38 41 97 🕐 Dinner only

PA AMB OLI (€€)

The name means 'bread and oil', a popular local snack served with platters of sausages, ham, grilled vegetables or grilled meat in this busy restaurant.
✉ Carrer Nou de Juliol 4 ☎ 971 38 36 19 🕐 Lunch, dinner Mon–Sat

RACÓ DES PALAU (€€)

Fish, pizzas and Italian cuisine is on offer here in the back streets behind the Palau Salord.
✉ Carrer des Palau 3 ☎ 971 38 54 02 🕐 Apr–Oct. Closed Sun lunch

RESTAURANT D'ES PORT (€€)

Fresh fish, seafood and grilled meats with a view of the fishing port. The main restaurant features lobster and fish from their own fishing boat, while the more informal brasserie has pizzas and a children's menu.
✉ Port de Ciutadella ☎ 971 48 00 22 🕐 Lunch, dinner

ROMA (€€)

Part of the Café Balear chain, the speciality here is pizzas cooked in a wood-fired oven.
✉ Carrer Pere d'Alcántara 18 ☎ 971 38 47 18 🕐 Closed Sun lunch

SA FIGUERA (€€€)

Grilled steaks and seafood dishes, including *caldereta de langosta*.
✉ Port de Ciutadella ☎ 971 38 21 12 🕐 Lunch, dinner

SA GELATERIA DE MENORCA (€)

The best ice cream in Menorca. Flavours include almond and cinnamon and fig. Also *granizado de limón* (lemon slush).
✉ Plaça de la Catedral 3 and Costa des Port 69 ☎ 971 38 11 92 🕐 Daily 10AM–2AM, summer only

SA LLESCA (€€)

Good for lunchtime snacks beneath the parasols on a lively old town square. Try the *llesca* – toast rubbed with tomato and topped with anchovies, ham, Menorcan sausages or Mahón cheese.
✉ Plaça Nova 4 ☎ 971 48 03 14 🕐 Daily 9–12 in summer

MENÚ DEL DÍA

Most restaurants offer a *menú del día* at lunchtime, and many in the evening too – a set-price three-course meal, with water or wine included. You won't get much choice (typically two or three choices for each course) but what you do get will be cheap, freshly cooked and filling. A full meal, with drinks, will usually cost about the same as a main course from the *à la carte* menu.

Where to Eat

Around the Island

VEGETARIANS

Vegetarians could have a hard time in Menorca – unless they eat fish. *Tapas* bars, however, usually have vegetarian options, including the ever-present *tortilla* (cold potato omelette), and Menorcan pizzas tend to be excellent, cooked the Italian way in a wood-fired oven. Two interesting vegetarian starters are *escalivada*, a mix of grilled vegetables in olive oil, and *tumbet*, a Mallorcan-style ratatouille with potatoes.

ALAIOR

THE COBBLERS (€€)
Fresh, imaginative Mediterranean cuisine in the garden of a typical Menorcan town house. Booking is essential.
✉ Costa d'en Macari 6
☎ 971 37 14 00 ⊙ Dinner Mon–Sat, Apr–Oct

BINIBECA VELL

EN CARAGOL (€€)
Fresh seafood and fabulous sea views from this popular summer terrace on the coast road between Binibeca and Punta Prima.
✉ Biniancolla, near Cala Torret
☎ 629 165089 ⊙ Lunch, dinner Tue–Sun, May–Oct

LOS BUCANEROS (€€)
Simple fish restaurant in a wooden shack on the beach. Very romantic.
✉ Platja de Binibèquer
☎ No telephone ⊙ Daily 10–8, May–Oct

BINIMEL-LÀ

BINIMEL-LÀ (€)
Pizzas, snacks, sandwiches and grilled meat in a windswept setting high above the beach.
✉ Platja de Binimel-là ☎ 971 359275 ⊙ Daily 10–7, May–Oct

CALA BLANCA

ES CALIU (€€)
A large and busy restaurant specialising in charcoal-grilled meats.
✉ Carretera Ciutadella–Cala En Bosc ☎ 971 38 01 65
⊙ Lunch, dinner, daily in summer; weekends only in winter

CALA EN BOSC

AQUARIUM (€€€)
Fresh fish and seafood from Menorca and Galicia – crayfish, prawns, turbot in *cava* – at this top-notch harbourside restaurant. The same owners have a Tex-Mex restaurant next door.
✉ El Lago ☎ 971 387442
⊙ Lunch, dinner daily, May–Oct

CAFÉ BALEAR (€€)
This branch of a well-known Ciutadella restaurant specialises in seafood, with dishes ranging from plain grilled lobster to anglerfish in almond sauce.
✉ El Lago ☎ 608 74 48 16
⊙ Lunch, dinner, summer

CA N'ANGLADA (€€)
Steaks, seafood and creative Mediterranean cuisine – a cut above the other places around the marina.
✉ El Lago ☎ 971 381402
⊙ Lunch, dinner Tue–Sun

CALA MACARELLA

SUSY (€€)
This summer restaurant beside the beach serves generous portions of Spanish cuisine such as grilled squid, grilled sole or roast chicken and chips.
✉ Platja de Macarella ☎ 971 35 94 67 ⊙ Daily 10:30–6, summer

CALA MESQUIDA

ES CAP ROIG (€€)
This is where the people of Maó come for a treat at weekends. Fresh fish and spectacular sea views.

Where to Eat

✉ Just before the village on the road from Maó ☎ 971 18 83 83 🕐 Tue–Sun, 11AM–midnight

CALA SANTA GALDANA

EL MIRADOR (€€)
Perched on a rocky outcrop above one of Menorca's prettiest bays.
✉ Over footbridge from Hotel Audax ☎ 971 15 45 03 🕐 Lunch, dinner

ES CASTELL

BUMERANG (€€)
Long-established fish restaurant in an ancient cave. *Paellas* and a good-value set lunch.
✉ Carrer Sant Josep 9 🕐 Lunch, dinner

CA'N DELIO (€€)
While away a summer evening eating fresh grilled fish beside the sea.
✉ Cales Fonts 38 ☎ 971 35 17 11 🕐 Lunch, dinner

DINKUMS (€€)
Fresh fish right on the harbourside in an old boathouse and cave, with a separate children's menu. The friendly English owner offers boat trips around Maó harbour at 3PM daily in summer.
✉ Cales Fonts 20 ☎ 971 367017 🕐 Lunch, dinner daily, May–Oct

EL ITALIANO (€€)
Classic Italian cooking in a country house – risottos, cheese fondues, pasta with truffles, Spanish and Italian wines. Children can ask for half portions.
✉ Carretera Sant Felip ☎ 971 36 53 10 🕐 Dinner only

ESPAÑA (€)
The locals come here for unpretentious Menorcan and Spanish food.
✉ Carrer Victori 48 ☎ 971 36 32 99 🕐 Lunch, dinner

LA CAPRICHOSA (€€)
Harbourside pizzeria with pasta, meat and fish dishes and a children's menu. Fish soup a speciality.
✉ Cales Fonts 44 ☎ 971 36 61 58 🕐 Lunch, dinner

SA VINYA (€€)
Wine, cheese and nibbles in a cave bar on the waterfront – just the place for an early-evening apéritif by the sea.
✉ Moll d'en Pons 7 ☎ 971 350384 🕐 Daily 6PM–1AM, Jun–Sep

SIROCO (€€)
Fresh fish served simply and well in a converted cave beside the harbour. Good-value *menú del día*. Separate children's menu.
✉ Cales Fonts 39 ☎ 971 36 79 65 🕐 Lunch, dinner

TRÉBOL (€€)
The best-known fish restaurant in Es Castell, and a night-time haunt of celebrities. Offers a sunny terrace or a shady cave.
✉ Cales Fonts 43 ☎ 971 36 70 97 🕐 Lunch, dinner

ES GRAU

TAMARINDOS (€€)
Simple fresh fish dishes and *paellas* beside the beach on a wooden terrace built directly over the sea.
✉ Pas d'es Tamarells 14 ☎ 971 35 94 20 🕐 Lunch, dinner

WINE

Most wines on offer in restaurants are imported from mainland Spain. The best red wines come from Rioja, made from the *tempranillo* grape and aged in oak – those labelled *crianza* are aged for at least a year, *reserva* for two, *gran reserva* for three. *Penedés* red and white wines from Catalunya are good value, as is *Cava*, Spanish sparkling wine, which comes from the same area.

Where to Eat

Around the Island

CALDERETA DE LANGOSTA

This thick lobster casserole, cooked with onions, tomato, garlic and parsley and served in an earthenware bowl, is the classic seafood dish of Menorca. It comes with thin slices of crispy bread to dip into the soup and a set of tools for tackling the lobster. The best place to eat *caldereta* is at Fornells, where each restaurant has its own recipe. It costs at least €50 per person; a cheaper alternative is *caldereta de mariscos* or *caldereta de peix*, with fish or seafood instead of lobster.

ES MERCADAL

CA'N AGUEDET (€€)
One of the best places on the island for traditional Menorcan cuisine.
✉ Carrer Lepanto 30 ☎ 971 37 53 91 ⏰ Lunch, dinner

CA'N OLGA (€€)
Authentic Menorcan and Mediterranean cooking in an intimate town house with a pretty summer terrace. Booking essential.
✉ Pont Na Macarrana ☎ 971 37 54 59 ⏰ Dinner, daily in summer; weekends only in winter

MOLÍ DES RECÓ (€€)
An old windmill at the top of the main street. In summer meals are served on the delightful terrace.
✉ Carrer Vicario Fuxà 53 ☎ 971 37 53 92 ⏰ Lunch, dinner

S'EIXERIT (€€)
Paella, grilled fish and a changing daily menu are served at this pretty garden restaurant in the centre.
✉ Carrer Tramuntana 29 ☎ 971 375308 ⏰ Lunch, dinner daily

ES MIGJORN GRAN

CA NA PILAR (€€)
Imaginative cooking (Mediterranean-style), with a garden terrace.
✉ Carretera Es Mercadal–Es Migjorn ☎ 971 37 02 12 ⏰ Lunch, dinner. Closed Wed

58 S'ENGOLIDOR (€€)
Fresh Menorcan cooking in an 18th-century town house with a terrace overlooking a gorge. Booking essential.
✉ Carrer Major 3 ☎ 971 37 01 93 ⏰ Dinner. Closed Mon

FERRERIES

BINISUES (€€€)
Traditional Menorcan cookery with an emphasis on fresh fish dishes served in an old manor house. Specialities include *caldereta de langosta*, crayfish with beans.
✉ Carretera Maó-Ciutadella, km 31 ☎ 971 373731 ⏰ Lunch, dinner daily in summer, weekends only in winter

EL GALLO (€€)
Charcoal grills are a speciality in this 200-year-old farmhouse. The steak with Mahón cheese is renowned.
✉ Carretera Cala Santa Galdana ☎ 971 37 30 39 ⏰ Lunch, dinner. Closed Mon

LIORNA (€€)
Arty pizzeria and restaurant; emphasis on modern Catalonian and Italian cuisine.
✉ Carrer Econom Florit 9 ☎ 971 37 39 12 ⏰ Dinner only. Closed Tue

FORNELLS

CA'N MIQUEL (€€)
Small restaurant on the promenade; speciality rice and fish dishes include local spiny lobster.
✉ Passeig Marítim ☎ 971 37 66 23 ⏰ Closed Sun dinner and all day Mon

CRANC PELUT (€€)
This restaurant at the end of the seafront promenade serves the usual lobster, *paellas* and fish dishes but also has a good selection

Where to Eat

of meat dishes.
✉ Passeig Marítim ☎ 971 37 67 43 🕐 Lunch, dinner, daily in summer

ES CRANC (€€€)
Local seafood; hidden away, so more popular with locals than tourists.
✉ Carrer Escoles 31 ☎ 971 37 64 42 🕐 Lunch, dinner. Closed Wed

S'ANCORA (€€)
One of the best of the fish restaurants directly facing the harbour.
✉ Passeig Marítim 8 ☎ 971 37 66 70 🕐 Lunch, dinner

SA LLAGOSTA (€€)
A short walk around the harbour from the main restaurant strip, this is intimate restaurant offers creative dishes like green squid risotto, duck with orange and steak with *foie gras* as well as the usual lobster casserole.
✉ Carrer Gabriel Gelabert 12 ☎ 971 376566 🕐 Lunch, dinner daily, May–Oct

SANT CLIMENT

ES MOLÍ DE FOC (€€€)
Sophisticated French and Spanish cuisine in a town house with a pretty garden.
✉ Carrer de Sant Llorens 65 ☎ 971 15 32 22 🕐 Lunch, dinner daily

SANT LLUÍS

ANAKENA (€€€)
Funky Mediterranean and international cuisine, including sushi, at a country house close to the gastro-village of Torret.
✉ S'Uestrà 90 ☎ 971 156727 🕐 Dinner only

BINIARROCA (€€€)
Elegant restaurant in a rural hotel offering fresh Mediterranean cuisine and seasonal produce from their organic gardens.
✉ Camí Vell de Sant Lluís ☎ 971 15 00 59 🕐 Dinner only. Closed Tue

EL PICADERO (€€)
British-run carvery and barbecue; very popular with expats for its Sunday lunch buffet.
✉ Carretera Maó–Sant Lluís ☎ 971 36 32 68 🕐 Closed Mon in winter

LA CARABA (€€)
One of the island's top restaurants offers modern Mediterranean cuisine in a country house with a summer terrace. Fresh fish and unusual meat dishes like *carpaccio* of ostrich with Mahón cheese.
✉ S'Uestrà 78 ☎ 971 15 06 82 🕐 Dinner Mon–Sat, Jun–Sep

PAN Y VINO (€€€)
British-run restaurant offering Menorcan and Mediterranean specialities in a charming village house. Booking essential.
✉ Torret 52 ☎ 971 15 03 22 🕐 Dinner only, Sat–Wed in summer

PEDRERA (€€€)
Creative French-Thai cooking; garden terrace.
✉ Torret 23 ☎ 971 15 07 17 🕐 Dinner only. Closed Mon

LA RUEDA (€€)
Tapas in the downstairs bar, Menorcan specialities in upstairs restaurant.
✉ Carrer Sant Lluís 30 ☎ 971 15 03 49 🕐 Lunch, dinner. Closed Tue

COFFEE

Most people drink *café solo* after a meal – short, strong and black, like an espresso. If you want your coffee with milk, ask for *café con leche*; *cortado* is a *café solo* with an extra dash of hot water. The waiter may bring you a glass of brandy or liqueur on the house; ask for a *carajillo* and your coffee will come with brandy already added.

Where to Stay

In Maó & Ciutadella

PRICES

Prices are for a double room, in summer, excluding breakfast and VAT:
€ = under €60
€€ = €60–€120
€€€ = over €120

These prices will be much lower if you book as part of a package holiday. Most hotels in the resorts are block-booked by tour operators and it is through them that you will get the cheapest deals.

MAÓ

CAPRI (€€)
Modern, comfortable, three-star hotel with a rooftop pool close to Plaça de S'Esplanada.
www.rtmhotels.com
✉ Carrer Sant Esteve 8
☎ 971 36 14 00 ⏰ All year

MIRADOR DES PORT (€€)
Three-star hotel with pool and sea views, 10 minutes' walk from the city centre.
✉ Carrer Dalt Vilanova 1
☎ 971 36 00 16 ⏰ All year

ORSI (€)
Small, old-fashioned, city-centre *hostal*.
✉ Carrer Infanta 19 ☎ 971 36 47 51 ⏰ Feb–Nov

PORT MAHÓN (€€€)
The best hotel in the capital, in an imposing colonial-style building overlooking the port. Fabulous gardens and a swimming pool.
www.sethotels.com
✉ Avinguda Fort de l'Eau 13
☎ 971 36 26 00 ⏰ All year

CIUTADELLA

CIUTADELLA (€)
Modest two-star *hostal* in an old terraced house five minutes' walk from the Plaça des Born.
✉ Carrer Sant Eloy 10 ☎ 971 38 34 62 ⏰ All year

ESMERALDA (€€)
1960s seaside hotel, by the Passeig Marítim. Most rooms have sea-facing balconies. Swimming pool, tennis courts and a children's play area.
www.mac-hotels.com
✉ Passeig de Sant Nicolau 171
☎ 971 38 02 50 ⏰ May–Oct

MADRID (€)
One-star hotel with a restaurant, swimming pool and garden, convenient for city centre and the sea.
✉ Carrer Madrid 60 ☎ 971 38 03 28 ⏰ May–Oct

OASIS (€)
Small, modest *hostal* near ring road with nine rooms around a central courtyard.
✉ Carrer Sant Isidre 33
☎ 971 38 21 97 ⏰ Apr–Oct

PARIS (€)
Simple rooms in an old-style Menorcan house on the edge of town, close to Cala des Degollador beach.
✉ Carretera Santandria 4
☎ 971 38 16 22 ⏰ Apr–Oct

PATRICIA (€€)
The best hotel in the city centre; popular with business people, and has minibars in every room and a swimming pool.
www.hesperia-patricia.com
✉ Passeig de Sant Nicolau 90
☎ 971 38 55 11 ⏰ All year

PLAYA GRANDE (€€)
Small, modern hotel beside the beach at Cala des Degollador. Balconies overlook the start of the Passeig Marítim.
✉ Carrer Bisbe Juano 2
☎ 971 38 24 45 ⏰ Feb–Dec

SANT IGNASI (€€€)
Former 18th-century summer house turned into a rural hotel with gardens, a pool and Anglo-Menorcan furniture.
www.santignasi.com
✉ Carrer Cala Morell ☎ 971 38 55 75 ⏰ Jan–Nov

Where to Stay

Around the Island

BINIBECA VELL

BINIVELL PARK (€€)
Houses and apartments are for rent in this purpose-built 'Mediterranean fishing village'.
✉ Urbanización Binibeca Vell
☎ 971 15 06 08 🕒 Apr–Oct

CALA D'ALCAUFAR

S'ALGAR (€€)
Modern four-star hotel with impressive facilities; most rooms have sea views.
✉ Urbanización S'Algar
☎ 971 15 17 00
🕒 May–Oct

SAN LUIS (€€)
Large three-star hotel overlooking the sea, with tennis and mini-golf.
✉ Urbanización S'Algar
☎ 971 15 07 50 🕒 May–Oct

XUROY (€€)
Charmingly old-fashioned *hostal* with its own landing stage right beside the beach at Cala d'Alcaufar.
✉ Cala d'Alcaufar ☎ 971 15 18 20 🕒 May–Oct

CALA DE SANT ESTEVE

SANT JOAN DE BINISSAIDA (€€)
Single, double and family rooms on a working farm with fabulous views. The French owner/chef cooks dinner using lamb, pork and vegetables from the farm.
www.binissaida.com
✉ Camí de Binissaida 108
☎ 971 355598
🕒 Apr–Jan

CALA EN BLANES

ALMIRANTE FARRAGUT (€€)
This massive hotel dominates the small cove of Cala En Forcat and has a pool, tennis courts, mini-golf and bike hire.
✉ Cala En Forcat ☎ 971 38 80 00 🕒 May–Oct

CALA EN BOSC

CALA'N BOSCH (€€)
Large hotel with rooms overlooking the sea and the usual facilities.
✉ Urbanización Cala En Bosc
☎ 971 38 70 00 🕒 May–Oct

LA QUINTA (€€€)
Five-star spa hotel in low-rise colonial-style buildings around a pool. Facilities include bike hire, golf practice area and health centre. A short walk from Son Xoriguer beach, and there are shuttle buses to Ciutadella.
www.laquintamenorca.com
✉ Carrer des Port ☎ 971 38 70 14 🕒 May–Oct

CALA EN PORTER

AQUARIUM (€€)
Modern three-star hotel with swimming pool and garden; by the beach.
✉ Urbanización Cala En Porter
☎ 971 37 70 77 🕒 May–Oct

CALA MACARELLA

MORVEDRA NOU (€€€)
Smart rural hotel, with 18 rooms; some in garden villas and others in the 17th-century house.
www.infotelecom.es/morvedra
✉ Camí de Macarella, 7km
☎ 971 35 95 21 🕒 May–Oct

HOTELS AND *HOSTALS*

All tourist accommodation in Spain is strictly classified and graded by the government. Hotels are graded from one to five stars according to facilities; *hostals*, with fewer facilities but often just as comfortable, are graded from one to three. At levels below three stars you may have to share a bathroom. Most hotels around the coast are closed throughout the winter; *hostals*, and hotels in the main towns, tend to stay open all year.

Where to Stay

Around the Island

PACKAGE HOLIDAYS

The cheapest accommodation in Menorca is available through tour operators and high-street travel agents, booked as part of a package deal with flights and perhaps car hire. As well as having access to cheaper rates at most hotels, many travel agents offer self-catering accommodation and 'agrotourism' holidays, staying in restored farmhouses and on country estates.

CALA MORELL

BINIATRAM (€€)
A 500-year-old farmhouse, with is own private chapel, on a working dairy. Tennis court and swimming pool.
www.infotelcom.es/biniatram
✉ Carretera de Cala Morell ☎ 971 38 31 13 🕒 All year

CALA SANTA GALDANA

AUDAX (€€€)
Luxury four-star beach hotel with a rooftop pool and sea-facing balconies. The sports centre can arrange everything from bike hire to scuba-diving.
www.rtmhotels.com
✉ Cala Santa Galdana ☎ 971 15 46 46 🕒 Mar–Oct

CALA GALDANA (€€)
Comfortable four-star hotel behind the beach near the Algendar gorge; pool, sauna and children's playground.
✉ Cala Santa Galdana ☎ 971 15 45 00 🕒 May–Oct

ES CASTELL

AGAMENÓN (€€)
Large, traditional seaside hotel with great views over Maó harbour.
www.sethotels.com
✉ Carrer Agamenón 16 ☎ 971 362150 🕒 Apr–Oct

ALMIRANTE (€€)
The former home of the British Admiral Collingwood is filled with paintings, maps and memorabilia of British rule. Good harbour views.
www.hoteldelamirante.com
✉ Carretera Maó–Es Castell ☎ 971 35 27 00 🕒 May–Oct

HAMILTON (€€)
Large, old-fashioned hotel in a quiet, central location. Swimming pool, gym and harbour views.
✉ Passeig Santa Agueda 6 ☎ 971 36 20 50 🕒 All year

MIRAMAR (€€)
This small two-star *hostal* beside the harbour is handy for walks along the Cala Figuera waterfront.
✉ Cala Fonduco ☎ 971 36 29 00 🕒 May–Oct

REY CARLOS III (€€)
Large three-star hotel with pool and garden overlooking the small harbour at Cala Corb.
✉ Miranda de Cala Corb ☎ 971 36 31 00 🕒 May–Oct

SON GRANOT (€€€)
Magnificent rural hotel in a restored 18th-century British mansion. Eight rooms, some with balconies and sea views.
www.songranot.com
✉ Carretera Sant Felip ☎ 971 355555 🕒 May–Oct

ES MERCADAL

JENI (€)
One-star *hostal* with a good Menorcan restaurant and a rooftop pool.
www.hostaljeni.com
✉ Carrer Mirada del Toro 81 ☎ 971 37 50 59 🕒 All year

ES MIGJORN GRAN

S'ENGOLIDOR (€€)
Four rooms in a family-run inn overlooking a gorge. The restaurant is one of the most celebrated in Menorca.
✉ Carrer Major 3 ☎ 971 37 01 93 🕒 May–Oct

FERRERIES

LOAR (€)
One-star apartment-hotel with its own pool.
www.hotel-loar.com
✉ Avinguda Verge del Toro 2
☎ 971 37 41 81 ◷ All year

SON TRIAY NOU (€€)
This pink colonial-style farmhouse is now a rural hotel with just four suites, plus a tennis court and swimming pool.
✉ Carretera Cala Galdana
☎ 971 15 50 78 ◷ Apr–Oct

FORNELLS

FORNELLS (€€)
Central three-star *hostal* with 17 rooms and a pool. Most rooms have balconies with sea views and the restaurant serves fresh fish and lobster.
✉ Carrer Major 17 ☎ 971 37 66 76 ◷ All year

PUNTA PRIMA

INSOTEL CLUB PUNTA PRIMA (€€€)
A five-star holiday village, with low-rise villas and gardens, tennis and squash courts, swimming pools, shops, restaurants, a health centre and children's clubs. The beach is about 300m away.
www.insotel.com
✉ Carrer Migjera ☎ 971 15 92 00 ◷ Apr–Oct

SANT CLIMENT

MATCHANI GRAN (€€€)
A large farmhouse restored by its British owners to offer luxury accommodation on a working sheep farm. Meals are served in a converted barn, and there is a heated outdoor pool. No children.
www.menorcacountryhouse.com
✉ Carretera Sant Climent–Binidali ☎ 971 15 33 00
◷ Apr–Oct

SANT LLUÍS

BINIALI (€€)
Eleven individual rooms in an old farmhouse with its own swimming pool in the countryside to the southwest of the town.
www.hostalbiniali.com
✉ Carretera S'Uestrà 50
☎ 971 15 17 24 ◷ Mar–Oct

BINIARROCA (€€€)
A 16th-century farmhouse lovingly restored and filled with art and antiques. Some of the 12 rooms have their own private garden and pool. A peaceful, child-free retreat.
www.biniarroca.com
✉ Camí Vell de Sant Lluís
☎ 971 15 00 59 ◷ Mar–Oct

SANT TOMÀS

SANTO TOMÁS (€€€)
Four-star hotel close to the beach, with 85 rooms and a large swimming pool.
www.sethotels.com
✉ Urbanización Santo Tomás
☎ 971 37 00 25 ◷ Apr–Oct

SON BOU

JARDÍN DE MENORCA (€€€)
Luxury four-star apartment-hotel in the resort of Sant Jaume Mediterrani.
✉ Urbanización Torre Solí
☎ 971 37 80 40 ◷ May–Oct

CAMPING

Menorca has two official campsites, at Son Bou (◷ Apr–Oct, ☎ 971 372727, www.campingsonbou.com) and S'Atalaia (◷ Jun–Sep, ☎ 971 373095), on the road from Ferreries to Cala Santa Galdana. The campsite at Son Bou is officially rated first-class and has a swimming pool and other sports facilities, as well as wood cabins and mobile homes for rent. Unofficial camping on Menorca's beaches is forbidden, and you may camp on farmland only with the owner's consent.

Where to Shop

Food & Drink

MARKETS

The two main food markets, in the Carmelite cloisters in Maó and Plaça Libertat in Ciutadella, are open every morning from Monday to Saturday. Most towns in Menorca also have a weekly market, with clothes and craft stalls set up around the main square. Market days are:
Maó – Tue, Sat
Ciutadella – Fri, Sat
Alaior – Thu
Es Castell – Mon, Wed
Es Migjorn Gran – Wed
Ferreries – Tue, Fri
A weekly farmers' market is held in the main square of Ferreries on Saturday mornings. Local farmers sell bread, cheese, honey and fresh produce and there are also pottery and craft stalls, and folk-dancing displays. Another craft market takes place on Thursday evenings in summer in Es Mercadal.

WHAT TO BUY

Good buys on the island include Mahón cheese, Xoriguer gin, Spanish wines and brandy, herbal liqueurs, almond biscuits and olive oil.

MAÓ

COLMADO LA PALMA
Delicatessen with Mahón farmhouse cheeses, Menorcan sausages, biscuits, gin and wines.
✉ Costa de Sa Plaça 15
☎ 971 36 34 63

EL TURRONERO
This shop has specialised in *turrón* (nougat) since 1894, and also sells Menorcan sausages, cheese and wine.
✉ Carrer Nou ☎ 971 362898

VALLÈS
Arty pastries and chocolate on Maó's upmarket shopping street.
✉ Costa de Sa Plaça 19
☎ 971 36 34 88

CIUTADELLA

BON GUST
Local wine, gin, cheese and sausages.
✉ Carrer Portal de Maó 20
☎ 971 484414

MIGUEL BAGUR
This pastry shop specialising in boxed *ensaimadas* and homemade biscuits.
✉ Carrer JM Quadrado 8 (Ses Voltes) ☎ 971 38 06 40

SES INDUSTRIES
Wines, liqueurs and cheese in olive oil are on offer in this Aladdin's cave near the cathedral.
✉ Carrer Santa Clara 4
☎ 971 38 28 82

ALAIOR

COINGA
The leading producer of Mahón cheese.
✉ Carrer Es Mercadal 8
☎ 971 37 12 27

QUESO BINIBECA
Mature goat's cheese and Mahón cheese sold from the farmhouse – signposted off the main road from Maó to Alaior.
✉ Carretera Maó-Alaior, km 5.5
☎ 971 369244

ES MERCADAL

CA'N PONS
Es Mercadal is known for its almond macaroons, and this is one of the best places to buy them.
✉ Carrer Nou 13
☎ 971 37 52 58

LOS CLAVELES
Pastry-shop specialising in Menorcan and Arabic-style biscuits and sweets. There is another branch by the main square in Ferreries
✉ Carrer Nou 31
☎ 971 15 40 64

FERRERIES

HORT DE SANT PATRICI
This dairy farm just outside Ferreries offers tastings of unpasteurised farmhouse cheese as well as a cheese museum and the chance to see Mahón cheese being made.
✉ Camino Ruma, 1km north of Ferreries ☎ 971 37 37 02

Where to Shop

Arts, Books & Gifts

The best hunting-grounds for unusual gifts are the boutiques along the waterfront in Maó and in the back streets of Ciutadella. Carrer Seminari in Ciutadella has small shops specialising in modern art, jewellery and antiques. There are a number of souvenir shops to be found alongside the Me-1 highway from Maó to Ciutadella.

ART AND CRAFTS

MAÓ

LORA BUZÓN
This pottery workshop will make items to order and ship them anywhere in the world. It also has 'ecological' T-shirts and cotton clothing.
✉ Moll de Ponent 10
☎ 971 36 35 85

S'ALAMBIC
Francesc Lora's pottery and a wide range of crafts and souvenirs are on sale at this waterfront shop.
✉ Moll de Ponent 36
☎ 971 35 03 03

ES CASTELL

S'ESCOPINYA
Harbourside boutique specialising in Lladró porcelain.
✉ Cales Fonts 1
☎ 971 36 76 92

ES MERCADAL

GALERIA DEL SOL
Art gallery featuring work by foreign artists in Menorca.
✉ Via Ronda 28
☎ 971 15 40 07

ES MIGJORN GRAN

GALERIA MIGJORN GRAN
Watercolours by the British artist Graham Byfield, who lives in the village, and by other local artists.
✉ Carrer Sant Llorenc 12
☎ 971 37 03 64

BOOKS

MAÓ

FUNDACIÓ
Here you'll find the best selection of books in Maó, including books on Menorca in English and German.
✉ Costa de Sa Plaça 14
☎ 971 36 35 43

GIFTS

ALAIOR

BALEARICA
A wide range of gifts, including shoes, bags and leather articles, at a large shop beside the main road. There are also branches in Maó, Ciutadella and Fornells.
✉ Carretera Maó-Alaior, km 15
☎ 971 372736

ES MERCADEL

SA FARINERA
The best of the large shopping emporiums that are strung out along the Maó to Ciutadella road. Set in an old flour mill, the complex includes an industrial museum as well as shops selling pottery, clothing and toys.
✉ Carretera Maó–Ciutadella, km20 ☎ 971 15 43 08
🕒 May–Oct, daily 10–8

OPENING HOURS

Most shops are open from around 10–1:30 and 5–8 Monday to Friday, and on Saturday mornings. Supermarkets are open 9–9 Monday to Saturday, while resort shops will usually stay open for long hours in summer.

Where to Shop

Leather & Jewellery

SHOES

Menorca's shoe industry was founded in the 19th century by Jerónimo Cabrisas, a businessman who emigrated to Cuba and returned to set up an export trade in shoes. At one stage, almost 40 per cent of the population was employed in shoemaking and the industry is still one of the most important on the island. Prices are good if you shop around, and the leather used in the best shoes is wonderfully soft and supple.

NATURAL DESIGNS

A recent trend in Menorca has been the arrival of natural cotton clothing, stonewashed and printed with offbeat designs reflecting the island's culture, ecology and fiestas. Two main companies, Pou Nou and Ecològica de Menorca, each produce a huge range of cotton T-shirts, along with dresses, shorts and hats which are sold across the island.

LEATHER

MAÓ

ES MACAR
This shop stocks one of the largest selections of Pou Nou cottonwear (▶ panel), with T-shirts, shorts, dresses, hats and beach gear all in funky local designs.
✉ Costa de Sa Plaça 50
☎ 971 365552

JAIME MASCARO
Maó branch of Menorca's best-known shoe manufacturer; the shop also sells leather jackets and bags.
✉ Carrer Ses Moreres 29
☎ 971 36 05 68

LOOKY
Leather and suede waistcoats, handbags, belts and locally made shoes.
✉ Carrer Ses Moreres 43
☎ 971 36 06 48

MARISA
Elegant boutique on Maó's smartest shopping street, with a fine selection of leather bags.
✉ Costa de Sa Plaça
☎ 971 36 27 63

MARK'S
Handbags, belts, suitcases and jackets are sold at two shops in the city centre.
✉ S'Arravaleta 18 and Costa de Sa Plaça 38 ☎ 971 36 26 60 and 971 36 56 25

PATRICIA
Quality shoes and other fashion accessories.
✉ Carrer Ses Moreres 31
☎ 971 36 91 78

RICCY
Upmarket boutique featuring high-class leather and jewellery.
✉ Carrer Nou 17
☎ 971 36 57 84

VIVES
Leather shoes and accessories.
✉ S'Arravaleta 16
☎ 971 36 28 46

CIUTADELLA

BLAU MARI
Fashionable shop in the vaults of the Palau Salord with shoes, espadrilles, leather articles and colourful T-shirts.
✉ Carrer Major del Born 11
☎ 971 48 10 95

CA SA POLLACA
This shop has been selling handmade leather shoes and sandals since 1897; they have a lovely selection of *abarcas* (rubber-soled sandals) for children.
✉ Carrer JM Quadrado 10
(Ses Voltes) ☎ 971 38 22 23

MUNPER
Huge factory shop on the outskirts of town selling good quality leather goods.
✉ Carretera Maó–Ciutadella, km42 ☎ 971 38 03 54

PATRICIA
The largest branch of Patricia's empire is found on the road out of town. Also town centre shops in Carrer Seminari and on the harbour steps.
✉ Carretera Cala Santandria
☎ 971 385056

PETIT PALAU
Bright, modern T-shirts

Where to Shop

and dresses, plus colourful *abarcas* (sandals), in the ground floor of the Palau Salord.
✉ Carrer Major del Born 7
☎ 971 383450

ES CASTELL

S'ABARCA
This workshop on the harbour steps produces handmade *abarcas* (Menorcan sandals). There is another branch in Maó.
✉ Baixada de Cales Fonts; also at Moll de Llevant 21, Maó
☎ 971 35 34 62

ES MERCADAL

G SERVERA
Old-fashioned craftsman producing the local sandals known as *abarcas*, with leather uppers and a sole made out of recycled rubber tyres. Get here early in your holiday and have shoes made to measure before you leave.
✉ Avinguda Metge Camps 3
☎ 971 37 53 84

FERRERIES

CALZADOS FERRERIAS
Ferreries is the centre of shoe production in Menorca and this shop sells the products of a local factory.
✉ Avinguda Verge del Monte Toro 36 ☎ 971 15 52 48

CA'N DOBLAS
Hand-made shoes and *abarcas* (sandals) at a traditional workshop beside the town hall and parish church.
✉ Plaça Jaume II 1 ☎ 971 155021

JAIME MASCARO
Large factory shop beside the Maó–Ciutadella highway, representing the best-known name in Menorcan shoes.
✉ Carretera Maó–Ciutadella
☎ 971 37 45 00

JEWELLERY

MAÓ

ANNA
Gold, silver, natural and artifical pearls are all on sale at this smart jewellery shop.
✉ Carrer Ses Moreres 46
☎ 971 36 33 83

JOIES DE LA MAR
Rita Pabst sells her own marine jewellery, with unusual designs incorporating seashells and coral, at this attractive harbourside boutique.
✉ Moll de Llevant 176 ☎ 649 238813

LOPEZ
A wide selection of silver and jewellery, including Majórica pearls from Mallorca.
✉ Carrer Ses Moreres 58 and 60 ☎ 971 36 04 78

CIUTADELLA

CARLES
Old-fashioned jewellers' shop in the heart of the old city.
✉ Carrer Santa Clara 16
☎ 971 38 07 34

JOYERÍA ANGLADA
Jewellery, silver, gold and Majórica pearls under the arches in Ses Voltes.
✉ Carrer JM Quadrado 23 (Ses Voltes) ☎ 971 38 15 48

COSTUME JEWELLERY

One of Menorca's leading industries is the manufacture of costume jewellery, using common metals which are coated with silver or gold and finished with imitation stones. The effect is to create something extravagant, yet without the expense of precious metal or gems. Most of the costume jewellery produced in Menorca is exported to South America, but there are still bargains to be had – especially at the annual fairs of costume jewellery, SEBIME, held in Maó's trade fair centre in April. (☎ 971 36 03 13).

Where to be Entertained

Art Galleries, Cinemas & Theatres

WHAT'S ON?

To find out what's on while you're staying, ask at your hotel or the tourist offices in Maó and Ciutadella, or check the listings in the daily paper *Menorca* and the English-language monthly *Roqueta*. In Ciutadella you can also look at the billboards which are displayed in Ses Voltes. Everything starts late – plays at around 9PM, films at 10, and music at any time up to midnight.

ART GALLERIES

MAÓ

SALA DE CULTURA LA CAIXA
A gallery in the heart of the pedestrian shopping quarter hosting temporary exhibitions of modern art.
✉ Carrer Nou 25 ☎ 971 35 30 62

SALA DE CULTURA SA NOSTRA
Art exhibitions in the former convent of Sant Antoni.
✉ S'Arraval 32
☎ 971 36 68 54

CIUTADELLA

ESGLÉSIA DEL ROSER
Occasional art exhibitions are held in this restored 17th-century baroque church.
✉ Carrer del Roser ☎ 971 38 10 50

MUSEU DEL PINTOR TORRENT
Collection of works by José Torrent.
✉ Carrer Rafel 11 ☎ 971 38 04 82

SALA DE CULTURA SA NOSTRA
Exhibition rooms and educational activities.
✉ Carrer Santa Clara 9
☎ 971 48 06 86

ES MERCADAL

GALERIA DEL SOL
Exhibitions of work by local and international artists are held here throughout the year.
✉ Via Ronda 28 ☎ 971 154007

ES MIGJORN GRAN

GALERIA MIGJORN GRAN
Exhibitions of work by British watercolour artist Graham Byfield and other local artists.
✉ Carrer Sant Llorenc 12
☎ 971 37 03 64 🕐 May–Sep Mon–Fri 10–1

CINEMAS

MAÓ

CINE ALCAZAR
✉ Carrer Santa Ana 27
☎ 971 36 34 06

CINE SALÓN VICTORIA
✉ Carrer Sant Roc 24
☎ 971 36 90 93

CIUTADELLA

CINEMA DES BORN
Films are frequently shown in this theatre.
✉ Plaça des Born
☎ 971 38 49 13

THEATRES

MAÓ

TEATRE PRINCIPAL
An elegant opera house with films, plays and a spring opera season. For the best views book a seat in one of the 80 boxes.
✉ Costa d'en Deià 46
☎ 971 35 57 76

CIUTADELLA

TEATRE MUNICIPAL DES BORN
The city's theatre in a 19th-century neo-classical building.
✉ Plaça des Born
☎ 971 38 49 13

Where to be Entertained

Music & Nightlife

Most of the late-night action in summer takes place in and around the big tourist resorts, where foreign-owned bars and pubs offer familiar accents and familiar beer. To meet locals head for some of the more established bars in the main towns. The main areas for nightlife are in Moll de Ponent in Maó (turn left at the foot of the harbour steps) and around Plaça de Sant Joan, behind the harbour in Ciutadella.

BARS AND CLUBS

MAÓ

AKELARRE
Waterfront bar attracting a sophisticated yachting crowd – laid-back music and occasional live jazz.
✉ Moll de Ponent 42 ☎ 971 36 85 20 🕐 8AM–4AM

ARS CAVA
Soul, jazz and Latin music at this cool cellar café near the market.
✉ Carrer d'Anunciavay 29 ☎ 971 363054

CAFÉ BAIXAMAR
Late-night meeting place of the young and trendy, on the waterfront.
✉ Moll de Ponent 17 ☎ 971 36 58 96 🕐 8AM–4AM

ICARO
Loud music and late-night *copas* (drinks) at one of the longest-established harbour bars.
✉ Moll de Ponent 46 ☎ 971 36 97 35 🕐 8PM–4AM

SALSA
Trendy nightspot with cool Latin sounds, close to the ferry port.
✉ Moll de Ponent 29 ☎ 971 352 996

CIUTADELLA

ASERE
Salsa club with Cuban music – go late.
✉ Port de Ciutadella ☎ 659 988 397 🕐 Summer, daily 11AM–4AM. Winter, weekends

JAZZBAH
Cool, late-night jazz bar behind the harbour.
✉ Pla de Sant Joan 3 ☎ 971 482953 🕐 Jun–Sep daily, 11PM–6AM, weekends only in winter

ES CASTELL

ES CAU
Bring your own instruments to this music bar, inside a cave. Folk music and fishermen's songs.
✉ Cala Corb 🕐 From 10PM

SANT CLIMENT

CASINO SAN CLEMENTE
Menorca's oldest jazz venue, with a large expat following. Visitors are encouraged to join in.
✉ Carrer Sant Jaume 2 ☎ 971 15 34 18 🕐 Jazz nights May–Oct, Tue 9:30PM–1AM

CASINO

MAÓ

CASINO MARÍTIM
Menorca's only casino has a terrace overlooking the harbour. Passports and smart dress are required.
✉ Moll de Llevant 288 ☎ 971 36 49 62 🕐 Daily 8PM–5AM

CLASSICAL MUSIC FESTIVALS

As well as Maó's spring opera season, there are international festivals of young musicians each summer in Maó and Ciutadella. Organ recitals are held daily from June to October in Maó's Santa Maria church, and a series of Easter concerts takes place in the main churches in Maó, Ciutadella, Alaior, Es Mercadal and Ferreries. Concerts are also held in summer in the cloisters and chapel of the Museu Diocesà in Ciutadella.

Where to be Entertained

Discos

COVA D'EN XOROI

This bar and disco is set inside a natural cave, high in the cliff-face above the sea. There are numerous stairways and rock platforms, and a dance floor precariously overlooking the sea. Open during the day for drinks, it turns into a disco at night and gets busy after midnight. There is an interesting Arabic legend attached to the cave (➤ 54).

By their very nature, discos come and go – what's in this year will already be *passé* by next, and changes of name and image are essential to keep the punters rolling in. Most of the larger resorts will have a disco of one kind or another, sometimes based in a hotel nightclub, and the only thing to do is to ask around or listen out for the disco beat. These are a few of the island's more established discos, or *salas de fiestas* ('party halls'). Most are open nightly throughout the peak tourist season, but only at weekends – if at all – in winter. They mostly get busy around midnight and stay open until around 6AM.

MAÓ

SI
Cool late-night spot with a name which means 'yes'. Or should that be yes, yes, yes...
✉ Carrer Verge de Gràcia 16 ☎ 971 36 00 04

CIUTADELLA

LATERAL
The old warehouses around the Pla de Sant Joan, the open space behind the marina, are home to numerous clubs and discos which get busy around midnight and continue well into the small hours. This is probably the best known. Just choose the music and the décor which suits your style – they change every year.
✉ Pla de Sant Joan 9 ☎ 971 38 53 28

CALA EN PORTER

COVA D'EN XOROI
Menorca's most unusual nightclub (➤ panel), with ambient chillout sunset sessions from 7PM each evening and a disco throughout the night, plus foam parties on Thursdays at 11PM.
✉ Urbanización Cala En Porter ☎ 971 37 72 36 ⓘ Summer: daily 10:30AM–9PM; disco 11PM–5AM

SON BOU

SAN JAIME
Part of the Club San Jaime complex in the neighbouring resort of Sant Jaume Mediterrani.
✉ Urbanización Sant Jaume ☎ 971 37 27 87

STREET PARTIES
Outdoor parties with discos and live music are a feature of all Menorca's main festivals (➤ 22). During the festival of La Verge del Gràcia in Maó (Sep), outdoor concerts are held each evening in various venues including Plaça de S'Esplanada, Plaça Miranda and the harbourside. These are a great way of meeting local people and soaking up the atmosphere of a Menorcan party. For details, check in the local paper or ask around at in the local bars. There are also occasional rock concerts at Maó's stadium, Polideportivo Municipal (☎ 971 36 76 61). You will find details in the local newspaper.

Where to be Entertained

Spectator & Participatory Sport

CRICKET

SANT LLUÍS

MENORCA CRICKET CLUB
The British expat community plays sides from the UK and the Balearics at weekends in summer. Tourists are welcome to watch or to join in with open games on Wednesdays and Saturday's in July and August. Check the programme on the website or in the monthly *Roqueta* magazine.
www.menorcacc.com
✉ Urbanización Biniparell, Sant Lluís (signposted from the Sant Lluís–Binidali road)

FOOTBALL

MAÓ

ESTADIO MAONÈS
Sporting Mahón play alternate Sundays, September to June.
✉ Carretera Sant Lluís ☎ 971 36 31 70

GOLF

SON PARC

CLUB SON PARC
Menorca's only golf course opened in 1977 and is being extended to 18 holes by summer 2005. Tuition is available and you can hire clubs and equipment. Facilities include a driving range, putting green, tennis courts and a restaurant. A handicap certificate is advised.
✉ Urbanización Son Parc ☎ 971 18 88 75 🕐 Daily

HORSE RACING

MAÓ/SANT LLUÍS

HIPÓDROMO DE MAÓ
Trotting races (▶ panel) all year: Saturday at 6PM (summer) and Sunday 10:30AM (winter).
✉ Carretera Maó–Sant Lluís ☎ 971 36 57 30

CIUTADELLA/CALA EN BLANES

HIPÓDROMO DE CIUTADELLA
Trotting races: Sunday, April to December.
✉ Torre del Ram, Cala En Forcat ☎ 971 38 80 38

HORSE RIDING
Horse and pony hire and excursions are available from:

ALAIOR

RUTES EQÜESTRES
☎ 971 154123

SANT CLIMENT

STABLES FARM
☎ 971 153200

SON PARC

HORT DE LLUCAITX
☎ 607 900999

MULTI-ACTIVITY

CALA SANTA GALDANA

AUDAX SPORTS AND NATURE
Activities from fishing to scuba-diving from beach hut beneath Hotel Audax.
✉ Passeig del Riu ☎ 971 15 45 48 🕐 Apr–Oct

TROTTING

Trotting has been popular in the Balearic Islands for at least 200 years; at one time neighbouring villages used to hold trotting races against each other. The jockey sits in a small cart behind the horse and has to prevent his horse from breaking into a gallop. A handicap system ensures that weaker horses get a head start on the others. The trotting races in Maó and Ciutadella at weekends make a great excuse for a family day out with a picnic – and a few bets on the side.

Where to be Entertained

Watersports

SAILING IN MENORCA

The calm waters around Menorca are perfect for sailing – there are no tides, few currents and the only real hazard is the *tramuntana* wind. There are long, sheltered bays at Maó, Fornells and Port d'Addaia and smaller inlets at Es Grau and Ciutadella; all of these are suitable for novice sailors but only experienced hands should tackle the open sea. You can charter yachts at any of the nautical clubs.

SAILING CLUBS AND MARINAS

MAÓ

CLUB MARÍTIMO
✉ Moll de Llevant 287
☎ 971 365022

CIUTADELLA

CLUB NÀUTIC
✉ Camí de Baix ☎ 971 383918

CALA EN BOSC

CLUB DEPORTIVO
✉ Marina Cala En Bosc
☎ 971 385238

ES CASTELL

CLUB NÀUTIC VILLACARLOS
✉ Cales Fonts ☎ 971 365884

FORNELLS

CLUB NÀUTIC
✉ Ses Salines
☎ 971 376328

PORT D'ADDAIA

CLUB NÀUTIC
✉ Marina Port d'Addaia
☎ 971 188871

SAILING TUITION

The following offer tuition in sailing and windsurfing. It is possible to hire catamarans and dinghies from these schools and also on some of the larger beaches.

CALA EN BOSC

SURF'N'SAIL MENORCA
✉ Platja Son Xoriguer
☎ 971 387105

FORNELLS

WINDSURF FORNELLS
✉ Carrer Rosari 169
✉ 971 188150

SCUBA DIVING

ARENAL D'EN CASTELL

LA SIRENA
✉ Hotel Castell Playa
☎ 971 358246

BINIBECA

CALA TORRET
✉ Cala Torret ☎ 971 188528

CALA BLANCA

DIVE CALA BLANCA
✉ Avinguda Cala Blanca
☎ 971 481414

CALA D'ALCAUFAR

S'ALGAR DIVING
✉ Urbanización S'Algar
☎ 971 150601

CALA EN BLANES

SEVEN FATHOMS
✉ Cales Picas
☎ 971 388763

CALA EN BOSC

BLUE WATER SCUBA
✉ Marina Cala En Bosc
☎ 659 574641

SUB MENORCA
✉ Platja Son Xoriguer
☎ 971 387834

CALA SANTA GALDANA

DIVING CENTER
✉ Hotel Sol Gavilanes
☎ 629 734873

Where to be Entertained

SUB MORENA
✉ Passeig del Riu 7
☎ 609 303760

CALA SANTANDRÍA

POSEIDON
✉ Hotel Bahia ☎ 971 382644

ES CASTELL

FLORIT SUB
✉ Carrer Gran 83 ☎ 971 365259

FORNELLS

DIVING CENTER
✉ Passeig Marítim 44B
☎ 971 376431

MENORCA DIVING CLUB
✉ Passeig Marítim 98
☎ 971 376412

PORT D'ADDAIA

BUCEO AVENTURA
✉ Marina Port d'Addaia
☎ 626 476778

ULMO DIVING
✉ Zona Comercial
☎ 971 359005

WATER-SKIING

Water-skiing is possible off some of the larger beaches in summer. Surf'n'Sail Menorca at Son Xoriguer (see Sailing Tuition) can arrange waterskiing. You can ski behind your own motor-boat, but it is essential to show respect to other sea-users. Water-skiing is forbidden in Maó and Ciutadella harbours.

WINDSURFING

Windsurfing boards and equipment are available for hire at several of the larger beach resorts in summer; ask at the beach bar or from the beach attendant hiring out sunloungers. Tuition is sometimes available. The sheltered coves and bays around the island create ideal conditions for beginners, especially in the Bay of Fornells. For windsurfing courses, contact the sailing schools listed above.

BEACH ACTIVITIES

Most of the larger beaches rent out equipment including pedaloes (pedal-boats), canoes, kayaks and jet-skis, or operate rides on a giant inflatable banana as it is towed at speed through the water. Make sure you wear a life-jacket and that children are protected.

SWIMMING

Most resort hotels have outdoor swimming pools and a few have heated indoor pools. Swimming in the sea is generally safe but beware of currents at remote coves and look for the safety flags at beaches manned by lifeguards. It is generally warm enough to swim in the sea from June to October. A few Menorcan beaches have been awarded the EU blue flag, which means that they are safe, clean and well-kept. Blue Flag beaches include Arenal d'en Castell, Cala Santa Galdana and Es Grau. For swimming outside the summer season, the municipal pools in Maó and Ciutadella are open all year.

DIVING IN MENORCA

The clear waters in many of Menorca's bays make for excellent diving. Besides the wealth of marine life, there are also numerous caves to explore and shipwrecks to discover off Cala Mesquida, Punta Natí and Son Bou. Diving is expensive – a single 'try dive' might cost €60 – and you are required to take out insurance. Remember, it can be dangerous to fly within 24 hours of diving.

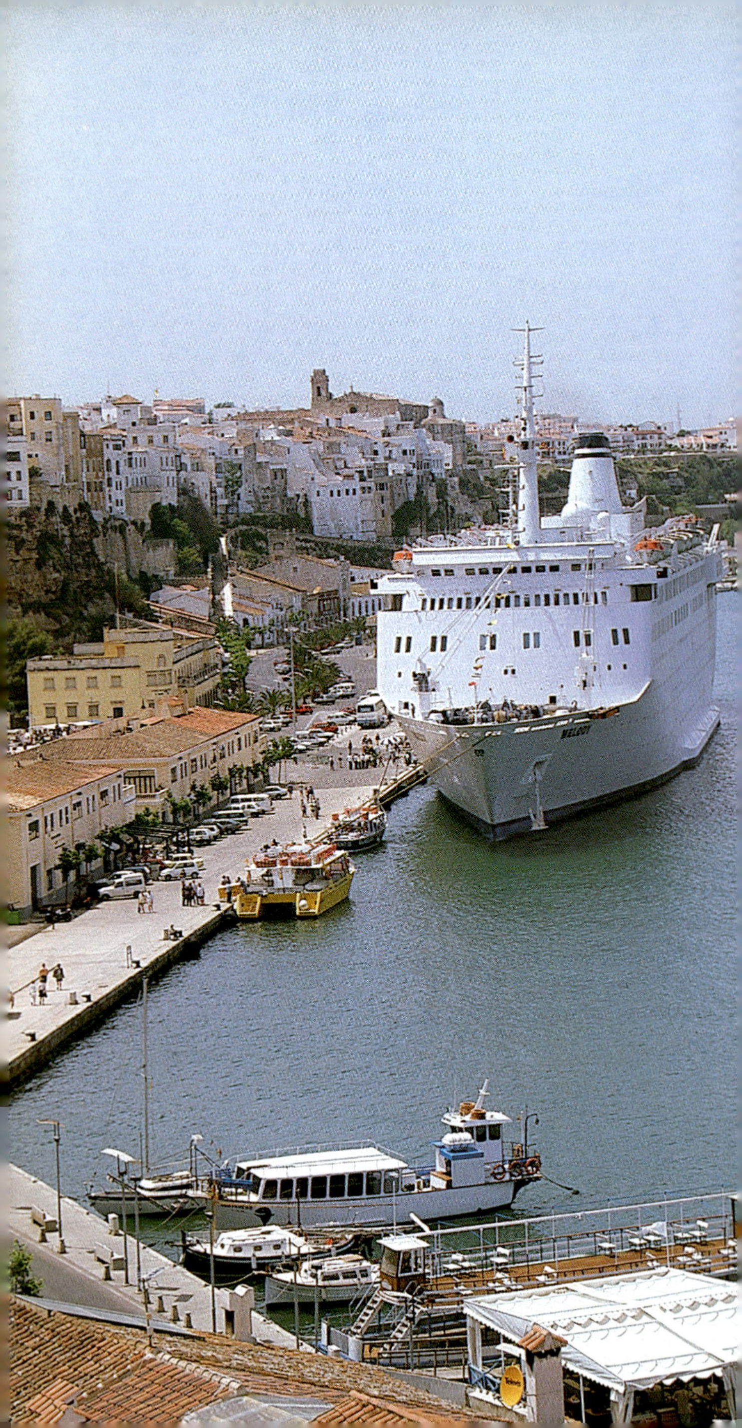

MENORCA
practical matters

BEFORE YOU GO

WHAT YOU NEED

- ● Required
- ○ Suggested
- ▲ Not required

Some countries require a passport to remain valid for a minimum period (usually at least six months) beyond the date of entry — contact the embassy or your travel agent for details.

	UK	Germany	USA	Netherlands	Spain
Passport/National Identity Card	●	●	●	●	▲
Visa (Regulations can change – check before your journey)	▲	▲	▲	▲	▲
Onward or Return Ticket	○	○	●	○	○
Health Inoculations	▲	▲	▲	▲	▲
Health Documentation (➤ 90, Health)	●	●	●	●	▲
Travel Insurance	○	○	○	○	○
Driving Licence (national with Spanish translation or International)	●	●	●	●	●
Car Insurance Certificate	●	●	●	●	○
Car Registration Document	●	●	●	●	○

WHEN TO GO

Menorca

■ High season
■ Low season

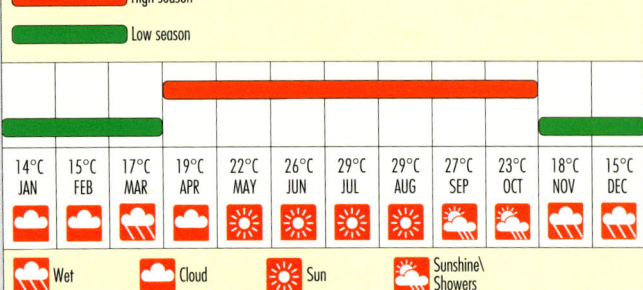

JAN	FEB	MAR	APR	MAY	JUN	JUL	AUG	SEP	OCT	NOV	DEC
14°C	15°C	17°C	19°C	22°C	26°C	29°C	29°C	27°C	23°C	18°C	15°C
Cloud	Cloud	Wet	Wet	Sun	Sun	Sun	Sun	Sunshine/Showers	Sunshine/Showers	Wet	Wet

Wet | Cloud | Sun | Sunshine\Showers

TIME DIFFERENCES

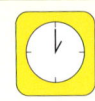

GMT	Menorca	Germany	USA (NY)	Netherlands	Rest of Spain
12 noon	1PM	1PM	7AM	1PM	1PM

TOURIST OFFICES

In the UK
Spanish Tourist Office
79 New Cavendish Street
London W1W 6XB
☎ 0207 486 8077
Fax: 0207 486 8034
www.spain.info

In the USA
Tourist Office of Spain
665 Fifth Avenue 35th
New York
NY 10103
☎ 212/265 8822
Fax: 212/265 8864
www.okspain.org

Tourist Office of Spain
8383 Wilshire Boulevard
Suite 956
Beverly Hills
CA 90211
☎ 323/658 7192
Fax: 323/658 1061

WHEN YOU ARE THERE

ARRIVING

Spain's national airline, Iberia (☎ 971 36 90 15), has scheduled flights to Menorca from the Spanish mainland and major European and North American cities, but most visitors arrive by charter plane. There are buses to and from the airport to central Maó every 30 minutes in summer and every 60 minutes in winter.

Maó (San Clemente) Airport to town centre — 5 kilometres

Journey times:
- 🚆 N/A
- 🚌 15 minutes
- 🚗 10 minutes

Maó Ferry Terminal in town centre

Journey times:
- 🚆 N/A
- 🚌 N/A
- 🚗 5 minutes

MONEY

The euro (€) is the official currency of Spain. Euro banknotes and coins were introduced in January 2002.
Banknotes are in denominations of 5, 10, 20, 50, 100, 200 and 500 euros and coins are in denominations of 1, 2, 5, 10, 20 and 50 cents and 1 and 2 euros.
Euro traveller's cheques are widely accepted, as are major credit cards. Credit and debit cards can also be used for withdrawing euro notes from ATM machines. Banks can be found in most towns in Menorca. Spain's former currency, the peseta, went out of circulation in early 2002.

TIME

Like the rest of Spain, Menorca is one hour ahead of Greenwich Mean Time (GMT+1), but from late March until late September, summer time (GMT+2) operates.

CUSTOMS

You may bring goods such as cigarettes and spirits into Menorca, from an EU country, for personal use, within these guidelines:
800 cigarettes, 400 cigarillos, 200 cigars, 1 kilogram of tobacco
10 litres of spirits (+22%)
20 litres of aperitifs
90 litres of wine, of which 60 litres can be sparkling wine
110 litres of beer

If you are bringing goods into Menorca from a non-EU country for your personal use, the allowances are:
200 cigarettes OR 100 cigarillos OR 50 cigars OR 250 grams of tobacco
1 litre of spirits (+22%)
2 litres of intermediary products (e.g. sherry) and sparkling wine
2 litres of still wine
50 grams of perfume
0.25 litres of eau de toilette
The value limit for goods is 175 euros.

Travellers under 17 years of age are not entitled to the tobacco and alcohol allowance.

NO
Drugs, firearms, ammunition, offensive weapons, obscene material, unlicensed animals.

CONSULATES

UK
☎ 971 36 33 73

Germany
☎ 971 36 16 63

USA
☎ 971 36 32 03

Netherlands
☎ 971 36 84 63

WHEN YOU ARE THERE

TOURIST OFFICES

Tourist Board
(Foment del Turisme de Menorca)

- Carrer Nord 4 – Maó
  ☎ 971 36 23 77
  Fax: 971 35 20 66

Tourist Information Offices
(Oficinas d'Informació Turística)

- Maó
  Sa Rovellada de Dalt 24
  ☎ 971 363790

- Port de Maó
  Moll de Llevant 2
  ☎ 971 355952

- Ciutadella
  Plaça de la Catedral 5
  ☎ 971 382693

- Fornells
  Carrer Major 57
  ☎ 971 376412

- Airport
  (inside arrivals terminal)
  ☎ 971 157115

These offices are typically open from Monday to Friday, 9:30–1:30 and 5–7, and on Saturday mornings from 9–1 though opening times may vary according to season. The office at Fornells is only open in summer while the airport office is open from 8AM–10PM daily between March and October. Each office can supply you with a free map of the island as well as information on accommodation, places to visit, transport timetables etc.

NATIONAL HOLIDAYS

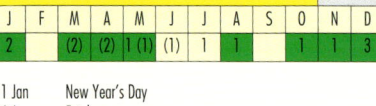

J	F	M	A	M	J	J	A	S	O	N	D
2		(2)	(2)	1 (1)	(1)	1	1		1	1	3

1 Jan	New Year's Day
6 Jan	Epiphany
Mar/Apr	Good Friday, Easter Monday
1 May	Labour Day
May/Jun	Corpus Christi
25 Jul	Saint James' Day
15 Aug	Assumption of the Virgin
12 Oct	National Day
1 Nov	All Saints' Day
6 Dec	Constitution Day
8 Dec	Feast of the Immaculate Conception
25 Dec	Christmas Day

Shops, banks and offices close on these days but in the main resorts many places remain open.

OPENING HOURS

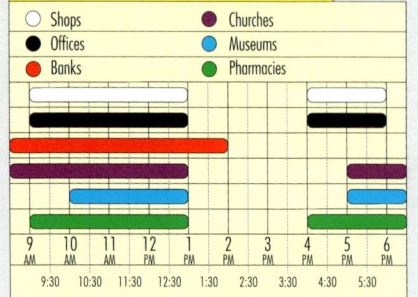

- ○ Shops
- ● Offices
- ● Banks
- ● Churches
- ● Museums
- ● Pharmacies

(9AM 10AM 11AM 12 1PM 2PM 3PM 4PM 5PM 6PM)
9:30 10:30 11:30 12:30 1:30 2:30 3:30 4:30 5:30

Large department stores, supermarkets and shops in tourist resorts may open outside these times, especially in summer. In general, pharmacies, banks and shops close on Saturday afternoon (although banks close all day Saturday from June to September). Banks stay open until 4:30PM Monday to Thursday, October to May.
The opening times of museums is just a rough guide; some are open longer hours in summer while hours are reduced in winter. Some museums close at weekends and/or Monday.

ELECTRICITY

The power supply in Menorca is: 220–225 volts.

Sockets accept two-pin plugs (round-pin style), so an adaptor is needed for most non-Continental appliances and a transformer for appliances operating on 100–120 volts.

TIPS/GRATUITIES

Yes ✓ No ✗		
Restaurants (if service not included)	✓	10%
Cafés/bars	✓	change
Tour guides	✓	€1
Hairdressers	✓	€1
Taxis	✓	10%
Chambermaids	✓	€1
Porters	✓	€1
Theatre/cinema usherettes	✓	change
Cloakroom attendants	✓	change
Toilets	✗	

WHEN YOU ARE THERE

PUBLIC TRANSPORT

Inter-Island Flights
Iberia operates several flights a day between Mallorca and Menorca (flight time: 30 minutes). There are no direct flights from Menorca to Ibiza (you are routed via Mallorca). Fares are inexpensive but you must book ahead at the height of summer (Iberia domestic flight reservations ☎ 902 40 05 00). For Maó airport information ☎ 971 15 70 00 (► 87, Arriving.)

Buses
Menorca has an extensive network of buses linking the main towns of Maó and Ciutadella with most coastal resorts and interior villages, supplemented by more intermittent local services between smaller towns and between neighbouring resorts. Destinations are marked on the front of the bus. Always check the time of the last bus back.

Inter-Island Ferries
There are sea services between Menorca and Mallorca. Trasmediterránea (☎ 971 36 60 50) operates a weekly car ferry between Palma and Maó (6 hours). There are also services twice daily between Ciutadella and Port d'Alcudia on Mallorca with Iscomar (☎ 971 48 42 16). For day-trips to Mallorca, Cape Balear (☎ 902 10 04 44) has a passenger-only fast catamaran service from Ciutadella to Cala Rajada (1 hour). Baleària (☎ 902 160180) also operate fast ferries between Ciutadella and Port d'Alcúdia (1 hour). Details of all these services can be found in *Menorca* newspaper.

Urban Transport
Only Maó and Ciutadella are large enough to have their own transport systems. In Maó local buses depart from the square across from the tourist office (► 88, Tourist Offices), however its narrow, congested streets make exploring on foot a better option. In Ciutadella local buses stop on Plaça S'Esplanada on the west side of the town centre.

CAR RENTAL

The leading international car rental companies have offices at Maó airport and you can book a car in advance (essential in peak periods) either direct or through a travel agent. Local companies offer competitive rates and will usually deliver a car to the airport.

TAXIS

Taxis can be hired at ranks (indicated by a blue square with a 'T'), on the street (by flagging down those with a green light) or at hotels. They are good value within Maó but expensive over long distances. A list of tariffs is displayed at taxi ranks.

CONCESSIONS

Students Holders of an International Student Identity Card (ISIC) may be able to obtain some concessions on travel, entrance fees etc, but Menorca is not really geared up for students, it is more suited to families and senior citizens. There are no youth hostels, but for cheap accommodation there are two campsites near Cala Santa Galdana and Son Bou.

Senior Citizens Menorca is an excellent destination for older travellers, especially in winter when the resorts are quieter, prices more reasonable and hotels offer very economical long-stay rates. The best deals are available through tour operators who specialise in holidays for senior citizens.

DRIVING

There are no motorways. The only main road links Maó and Ciutadella (speed limit: **90kph**)

Speed limit on minor roads: **40kph**

Speed limit on urban roads: **40kph**

Seat belts must be worn at all times. Children under 12 must use a child seat.

Random breath-testing. Never drive under the influence of alcohol.

All hire cars take either unleaded petrol (*sin plomo*) or diesel (*gasoleo*). There are 24-hour petrol stations in Maó, Ciutadella, Sant Lluís and on the C721 highway at Alaior and Es Mercadal. There are few petrol stations away from the main highway, though there is one close to Son Parc on the Maó to Fornells road. Most stations accept credit cards.

If you break down driving your own car and are a member of an AIT-affiliated motoring club, you can call the Real Automóvil Club de España (☎ 900 118118). If the car is hired follow the instructions given in the documentation; most of the international rental firms provide a rescue service.

PHOTOGRAPHY

What to photograph: prehistoric monuments (*talaiots*), secluded coves (*calas*), the old town areas of Maó and Ciutadella.
Best time to photograph: the powerful Menorcan summer sun can make photos taken at the height of the day appear 'flat'; it is best to photograph in the early morning or late evening.
Film and camera batteries are available from shops and *drouguerías*.

WHEN YOU ARE THERE

PERSONAL SAFETY

The national police force, the Policía Nacional keep law and order in urban areas. Some resorts have their own tourist-friendly Policía Turística. If you need a police station ask for *la comisaría*.

To help prevent crime:
- Do not carry more cash than you need.
- Do not leave valuables on the beach or poolside.
- Beware of pickpockets in markets, tourist sights or crowded places.
- Avoid walking alone in dark alleys at night.

Police assistance:
☎ **112**
from any call box

TELEPHONES

Most public telephones accept coins, credit cards and phonecards (*tarjetas teléfonicas*), which can be bought at post offices, kiosks and *tabacos*. All telephone numbers in the Balearic Islands have the same code (971), and you need to dial this code even when calling from within Menorca. Most European mobile phones work well in Menorca.

International Dialling Codes	
From Menorca (Spain) to:	
UK:	00 44
Germany:	00 49
USA:	00 1
Netherlands:	00 31

POST

Post Offices

Máo
Carrer Bonaire 15 🕒 Mon–Sat 8:30–8:30

Ciutadella
Plaça des Born 9 🕒 Mon–Fri 8:30–8:30. Sat 9:30–1
Stamps are also available from tobacconists and postcard shops

HEALTH

Insurance
Nationals of EU and certain other countries can get medical treatment in Spain with the relevant documentation (Form E111 for Britons), although private medical insurance is still advised and is essential for all other visitors.

Dental Services
Dental treatment is not usually available free of charge as all dentists practise privately. A list of *dentistas* can be found in the yellow pages of the telephone directory. Dental treatment should be covered by private medical insurance.

Sun Advice
The sunniest (and hottest) months are July and August, with an average of 11 hours sun a day and daytime temperatures of 29°C. Particularly during these months you should avoid the midday sun and use a strong sunblock.

Drugs
Prescription and non-prescription drugs and medicines are available from pharmacies (*farmàcias*), distinguished by a large green cross. They are able to dispense many drugs which would be available only on prescription in other countries.

Safe Water
Tap water is generally safe though it can be heavily chlorinated. Mineral water is cheap to buy and is sold as *con gaz* (carbonated) and *sin gaz* (still). Drink plenty of water during hot weather.

WHEN YOU ARE THERE

LANGUAGE

The language that you hear on the streets is most likely to be Menorquín, a version of Catalan, which itself shares features with both French and Spanish but sounds nothing like either and is emphatically a language, not a dialect. Catalan and Spanish both have official status on Menorca, and though Spanish will certainly get you by (it is still the language used by Menorcans to address strangers), it is useful to know some Catalan if only to understand all those street signs which are being slowly replaced by signs in Catalan.

English	Catalan	English	Catalan
hotel	hotel	chambermaid	cambrera
bed and breakfast	llit i berenar	bath	bany
single room	habitació senzilla	shower	dutxa
double room	habitació doble	toilet	toaleta
one person	una persona	balcony	balcó
one night	una nit	key	clau
reservation	reservas	lift	ascensor
room service	servei d'habitació	sea view	vista al mar
bank	banc	credit card	carta de crèdit
exchange office	oficina de canvi	exchange rate	tant per cent
post office	correus	commission charge	comissió
coin	moneda	cashier	caixer
banknote	bitllet de banc	change	canvi
cheque	xec	foreign currency	moneda estrangera
traveller's cheque	xec de viatge		
café	cafè	starter	primer plat
pub/bar	celler	main course	segón plat
breakfast	berenar	dessert	postres
lunch	dinar	bill	cuenta
dinner	sopar	beer	cervesa
table	mesa	wine	vi
waiter	cambrer	water	aigua
waitress	cambrera	coffee	cafè
aeroplane	avió	single ticket	senzill-a
airport	aeroport	return ticket	anar i tornar
train	tren	non-smoking	no fumar
bus	autobús	car	cotxe
station	estació	petrol	gasolina
boat	vaixell	bus stop	la parada
port	port	how do I get to...?	per anar a...?
ticket	bitlet	where is...?	on és...?
yes	si	you're welcome	de res
no	no	how are you?	com va?
please	per favor	do you speak English?	parla anglès?
thank you	gràcies	I don't understand	no ho entenc
welcome	de res	how much?	quant es?
hello	hola	open	obert
goodbye	adéu	closed	tancat
good morning	bon dia	today	avui
good afternoon	bona tarda	tomorrow	demà
goodnight	bona nit		
excuse me	perdoni		

WHEN DEPARTING

REMEMBER

- Contact your airline on the day prior to leaving to ensure the flight details are unchanged.
- You should check in at least 60 minutes before your flight.
- If travelling by ferry you must check in no later than the time specified on the ticket.

Index

A
accommodation 70–73
agrotourism 72
airport 87, 89
Ajuntament de Maó 59
Alaior 17, 24
Alfonso III of Aragón 9
Algendar Gorge 21, 25
Aquapark 56
Arenal d'en Castell 54
Arenal de Son Saura 28, 50
arriving 87
art and crafts 75
art galleries 78
Ateneu de Maó 59

B
Balearic Islands 8
Barranc d'Algendar 21, 25
bars and clubs 79
Bastió de Sa Font 35
beach resorts 54
beaches 50, 54, 57, 83
Binibeca Vell 17, 26
Binibèquer Nou 26
Binimel-là 31
birdwatching 21, 25, 46
boat tours 42, 46, 57
bookshops 75
buses 89

C
Cala d'Alcaufar 51, 57
Cala d'Algaiarens 27
Cala Blanca 57
Cala En Bosc 54
Cala En Porter 57
Cala En Turqueta 28
Cala Escorxada 50
Cala Macarella 29
Cala Macarelleta 29
Cala Mesquida 54
Cala Mitjana 50
Cala Morell 30
Cala del Pilar 50
Cala Pregonda 31
Cala de Sa Torreta 18
Cala de Sant Esteve 51
Cala Santa Galdana 25, 32, 57
Cala des Talaier 28
Cala Trebalúger 50
caldereta de langosta 12, 39, 68
Cales Coves 33
Cales Fonts 7, 16
Camí de Cavalls 20
Camí d'en Kane 19
camping 73
Cap de Cavallería 51
Cap de Favàritx 51
car rental 89
Castell Sant Antoni 39
Castell Sant Nicolau 59
Cathedral, Ciutadella 52
caves 29, 30, 33, 37, 47, 54, 80
cheese-making 24
children's attractions 56–57
Christian basilica 47
Cifuentes, Count of 6, 34
cinemas 78
Ciutadella 6, 7, 12, 15, 34–36, 52, 53, 59
climate 8
Club Escola Menorquina 56
Club San Jaime 56
concessions 89
consulates 87
costume jewellery 77
Cova d'en Xoroi 54, 80
Cova des Coloms 37
cricket 81
customs 87

D
dairy farming 7
discos 80
diving 82–83
drives
  Camí d'en Kane 19
  Ciutadella to Maó 15
  southeastern Menorca 17
driving in Menorca 89

E
eating out 57, 60, 62–69
electricity 88
entertainment 78–83
Es Castell 16, 53
Es Fornàs de Torelló 55

Es Grau 18, 46, 57
Es Mercadal 53
Es Migjorn Gran 37
Es Prego 31
Església del Carme 41

F
Ferreries 15, 38
ferries 89
festivals and events 12, 22
Flat Island 42
Fondeadero de los Llanes 18
food and drink 7, 64, 66, 67, 68, 69
  shopping for 74
  see also eating out
football 81
Fornells 12, 19, 39
Fortalesa de la Mola 52
Fort Marlborough 51
Fort Sant Felip 42, 52
free attractions 59

G
geography 8
gifts and souvenirs 75
gin distillery 59
Golden Farm 42
golf 81

H
Harbour, Maó 12, 42
health 86, 90
history of Menorca 10–11
horse riding 56–57, 81
horse-racing 81
Hort de Llucaitx Park 56
hostals 71
Hotel del Almirante 42
hotel grades 71

I
Illa d'en Colom 46
Illa Plana 42
Illa del Rei 42

K
Kane, Sir Richard 9, 19, 59
King's Island 42

Index

L
La Mola 42
language 8, 91
Lazareto 42
leather goods 76–77
limestone gorges 20, 25
lobsters 39, 68

M
Maó 6, 7, 12, 14, 15, 40–43, 52, 59
markets 74
menú del día 65
Mirador de Sa Punta 32
money 87
Monte Toro 8, 12, 20, 44
Museu de la Natura 38
Museu de Menorca 55
Museu Municipal 35
Museu del Pintor Torrent 59
music festivals 79

N
national holidays 88
Naveta des Tudons 45
navetas 21, 45
Nelson, Lord 42
nightlife 79
nude bathing 29

O
opening hours 63, 75, 88
Orfila, Mateu 9
Ostriches de Menorca 57

P
package holidays 72
Palau Salord 52
Passeig Marítim, Ciutadella 53
passports 86
pedaloes 57, 83
personal safety 90
photography 89
Picadero Menorca 57
Plaça des Born, Ciutadella 36
Plaça de S'Esplanada, Maó 14, 43
Platja d'es Tancats 27

police 90
Pons, Joan 9
population 8
Post Offices 90
prehistoric sites 17, 21, 30, 33, 45, 47, 48, 55, 58, 59
public transport 89

R
restaurants 57, 60, 62–69
road trains 56

S
sailing 82
St Stephen's Creek 51
S'Albufera des Grau 21, 46
S'Albufera National Park 46
salt-water marshes 46
sandstone quarry 58
Sant Agustí Vell 58
Sant Antoni 42
Sant Diego Church 24
Sant Jaume Mediterrani 47
Sant Lluís 53
Sant Tomàs 54
Santa Agueda 20, 51
Santa Eulàlia Church 24
Santa Maria Church 52
Sa Penya de S'Indio 15
Sa Torreta 18, 58
S'Enclusa 38
senior citizens 89
Ses Voltes, Ciutadella 53
shoe industry 38, 76
shopping 74–77
S'Hostal 58
Son Bou 47, 57
Son Catlar 55
Son Mercer de Baix 38
Son Parc 54, 57
Son Xoriguer 54
sports 81–83
street parties 80
students 89
sun protection 56, 90
swimming 83

T
Talaiotic culture 6, 35, 48, 55, 58

talaiots 21, 48, 55, 58
Talatí de Dalt 55
tapas 64, 66
taulas 12, 21, 48, 55, 58
taxis 89
telephones 90
theatres 78
time 86, 87
tips and gratuities 88
Torre de Fornells 39
Torelló 55
Torralba d'en Salord 55
Torre d'en Galmés 48
Torrent, José 59
tourism 8
tourist offices 86, 88
travel documents 86
Trepucó 55
trotting races 12, 81

U
Unesco Biosphere Reserve 7, 46

V
vegetarian food 66
viewpoints 51
visas 86

W
walking 20
walks
  from Es Castell 16
  Maó 14
  to Sa Torreta 18
water-skiing 83
watersports 82–83
weather 8, 86
wild flowers 21
wildlife 25, 46
windmill 53
windsurfing 83
wines 67

X
Xoriguer 59
Xoroi 54

TwinPack
Menorca

Written and updated by Tony Kelly
Edited, designed and produced by AA Publishing

Published by AA Publishing, a trading name of Automobile Association Developments Limited, whose registered office is Southwood East, Apollo Rise, Farnborough, Hampshire, GU14 0JW. Registered number 1878835.

The contents are believed correct at the time of printing. Nevertheless, the publishers cannot be held responsible for any errors or omissions or for changes in the details given in this guide or for the consequences of any reliance on the information it provides. This does not affect your statutory rights. Assessments of attractions, hotels, restaurants and other sights are based upon the author's personal experience and, therefore, necessarily contain elements of subjective opinion which may not reflect the publishers' opinion or dictate a reader's own experiences on another occasion.

We have tried to ensure accuracy in this guide, but things do change and we would be grateful if readers would advise us of any inaccuracies they may encounter.

All rights reserved. No part of this publication may be reproduced, stored in a retrieval system, or transmitted in any form or by any means – electronic, photocopying, recording, or otherwise – unless the written permission of the publishers has been obtained beforehand. This book may not be lent, resold, hired out or otherwise disposed of by way of trade in any form of binding or cover other than that in which it is published, without the prior consent of the publishers.

Material in this book may have appeared in other AA publications.

© **AUTOMOBILE ASSOCIATION DEVELOPMENTS LIMITED 2000, 2002, 2005**
First published 2000
Revised second edition 2002
Reprinted Oct 2003
Revised third edition 2005

A CIP catalogue record for this book is available from the British Library.

ISBN-10: 0 7495 4343 4
ISBN-13: 978 0 7495 4343 3

Colour separation by Keenes, Andover
Printed and bound by Times Publishing Limited, Malaysia

ACKNOWLEDGEMENTS
All pictures used in this publication are held in the Association's own library (AA PHOTO LIBRARY) and were taken by James Tims with the exception of the following: Peter Baker 90c; Ken Paterson front cover (a) lilo, (g) flowers, 90b; Roy Victor front cover (b) cocktail

A02011
Fold out map © Freytag–Berndt u. Artaria KG, 1231 Vienna–Austria, all rights reserved

TITLES IN THE TWINPACK SERIES
• Algarve • Corfu • Costa Blanca • Costa del Sol • Cyprus • Gran Canaria •
• Lanzarote & Fuerteventura • Madeira • Mallorca • Malta & Gozo • Menorca • Tenerife •

Dear **TwinPack** Traveller

Your comments, opinions and recommendations are very important to us. So please help us to improve our travel guides by taking a few minutes to complete this simple questionnaire.

You do not need a stamp (unless posted outside the UK). If you do not want to cut this page from your guide, then photocopy it or write your answers on a plain sheet of paper.

Send to: **The Editor, AA TwinPack Travel Guides, FREEPOST SCE 4598, Basingstoke RG21 4GY.**

Your recommendations…

We always encourage readers' recommendations for restaurants, nightlife or shopping – if your recommendation is used in the next edition of the guide, we will send you a *FREE* **AA TwinPack Guide** of your choice. Please state below the establishment name, location and your reasons for recommending it.

_____
_____
_____

Please send me **AA TwinPack**
Algarve ❏ Corfu ❏ Costa Blanca ❏ Costa del Sol ❏ Cyprus ❏
Gran Canaria ❏ Lanzarote & Fuerteventura ❏ Madeira ❏
Mallorca ❏ Malta & Gozo ❏ Menorca ❏ Tenerife ❏
(*please tick as appropriate*)

About this guide…

Which title did you buy?
  AA *TwinPack* _____
Where did you buy it? _____
When? m m / y y

Why did you choose an AA *TwinPack* Guide? _____
_____
_____
_____

Did this guide meet your expectations?
  Exceeded ❏ Met all ❏ Met most ❏ Fell below ❏
  Please give your reasons _____
_____
_____

continued on next page…

Were there any aspects of this guide that you particularly liked? _____

_____

_____

Is there anything we could have done better? _____

_____

_____

About you...

Name (*Mr/Mrs/Ms*) _____

Address _____

_____

_____ Postcode _____

Daytime tel no _____

Please only give us your mobile phone number if you wish to hear from us about other products and services from the AA and partners by text or mms.

Which age group are you in?
Under 25 ☐   25–34 ☐   35–44 ☐   45–54 ☐   55–64 ☐   65+ ☐

How many trips do you make a year?
Less than one ☐   One ☐   Two ☐   Three or more ☐

Are you an AA member? Yes ☐   No ☐

About your trip...

When did you book? m m / y y   When did you travel? m m / y y

How long did you stay? _____

Was it for business or leisure? _____

Did you buy any other travel guides for your trip?

If yes, which ones? _____

Thank you for taking the time to complete this questionnaire. Please send it to us as soon as possible, and remember, you do not need a stamp (*unless posted outside the UK*).

Happy Holidays!

The information we hold about you will be used to provide the products and services requested and for identification, account administration, analysis, and fraud/loss prevention purposes. More details about how that information is used is in our privacy statement, which you'll find under the heading "Personal Information" in our terms and conditions and on our website: www.theAA.com. Copies are also available from us by post, by contacting the Data Protection Manager at AA, Southwood East, Apollo Rise, Farnborough, Hampshire GU14 0JW.

We may want to contact you about other products and services provided by us, or our partners (by mail, telephone) but please tick the box if you DO NOT wish to hear about such products and services from us by mail or telephone. ☐